25.12

C.

CW00601736

Other titles in this series:
The World's Greatest Business Cartoons
The World's Greatest Cat Cartoons
The World's Greatest Computer Cartoons
The World's Greatest Dad Cartoons
The World's Greatest Golf Cartoons
The World's Greatest Keep Fit Cartoons
The World's Greatest Middle Age Cartoons

Published simultaneously in 1994 by Exley Publications in Great Britain and Exley Giftbooks in Ihc USA.

Selection © Exley Publications Ltd.
The copyright for each cartoon remains with the cartoonist.

ISBN 1-85015-509-7

A copy of the CIP data is available from the British Library on request.

Front cover illustration by Roland Fiddy.
Designed by Pinpoint Design.
Edited by Mark Bryant.
Printed and bound by Grafo, S.A., Bilbao, Spain.

Exley Publications Ltd, 16 Chalk Hill, Watford, Herts WD1 4BN, UK.
Exley Giftbooks, 232 Madison Avenue, Suite 1206, NY 10016, USA.

## THANK YOU

We would like to thank all the cartoonists who submitted entries for The World's Greatest DO-IT-YOURSELF CARTOONS. They came in from many parts of the world – including Spain, Israel, Italy, Japan, Mexico and New Zealand.

Special thanks go to the cartoonists whose work appears in the final book. They include Sally Artz page 54; Ros Asquith pages 6, 15, 26, 31, 43, 53, 56, 60, 62, 66, 77; Clive Collins page 34; Stidley Easel pages 10, 18, 22, 27, 33, 37, 42, 58, 65; Roland Fiddy cover, title page and pages 4, 16, 24, 30, 38, 50, 52, 55, 61, 72, 74, 76; Fleo page 13; Noel Ford pages 9, 20, 32, 36, 46, 51, 69, 75, 79; Xaquin Marin Formoso page 35; Martin Honeysett page 44; Tony Husband pages 5, 12, 19, 25, 41, 47, 64, 68, 73; Mik Jago page 70; Larry pages 11, 14, 23, 29, 39, 57, 63, 71, 78; Kenji Morita page 45; David Myers pages 8, 21; Sergio Navarro page 48; Bryan Reading pages 7, 17, 28, 40, 59; Bill Stott pages 49, 67.

Every effort has been made to trace the copyright holders of cartoons in this book. However any error will gladly be corrected by the publisher for future printings.

THE WORLD'S GREATEST

# DO-IT-YOURSELF CARTOONS

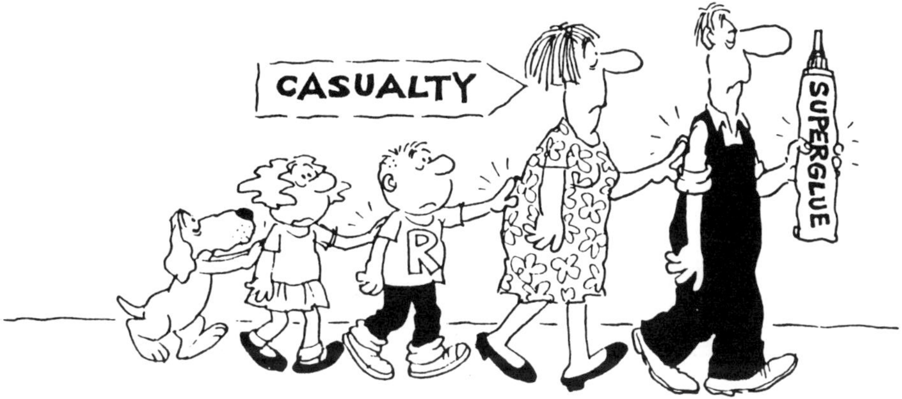
CASUALTY
SUPERGLUE

EDITED BY
**Mark Bryant**

EXLEY
NEW YORK • WATFORD, UK

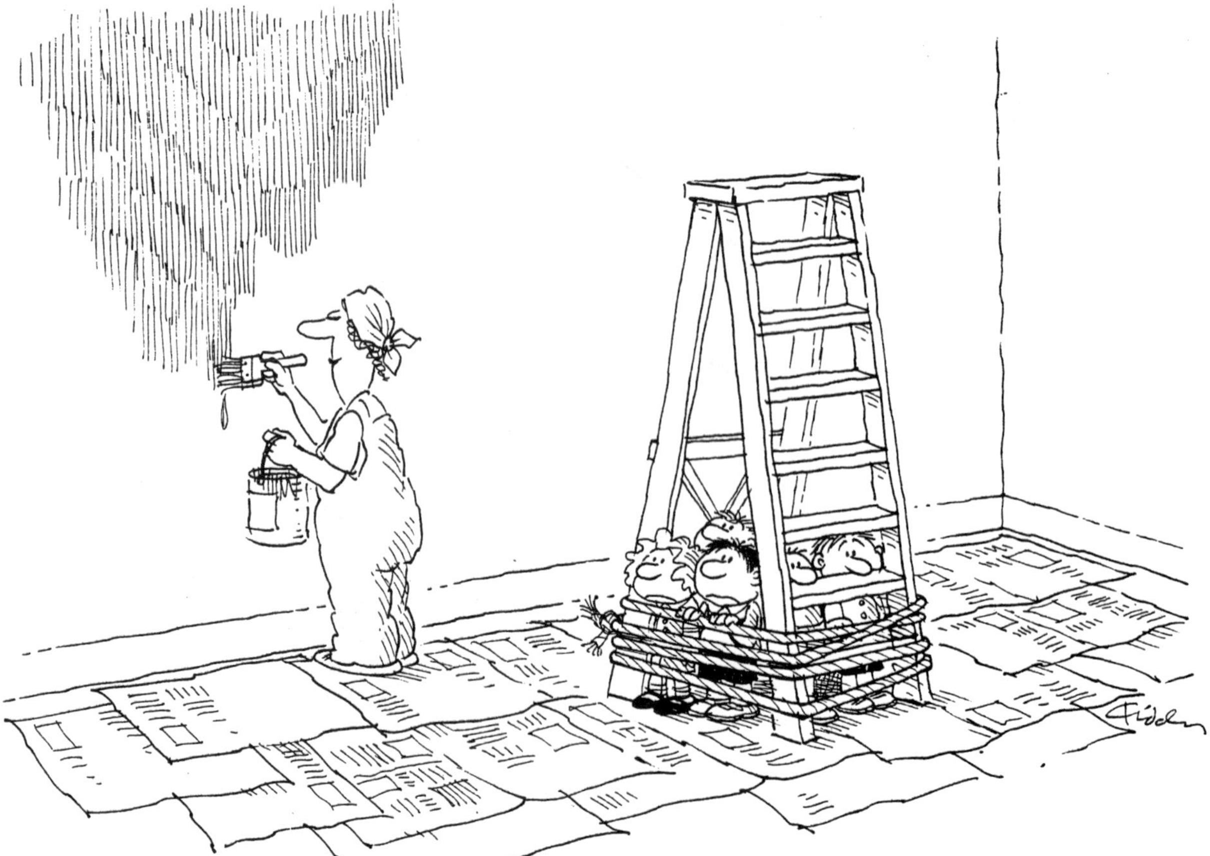

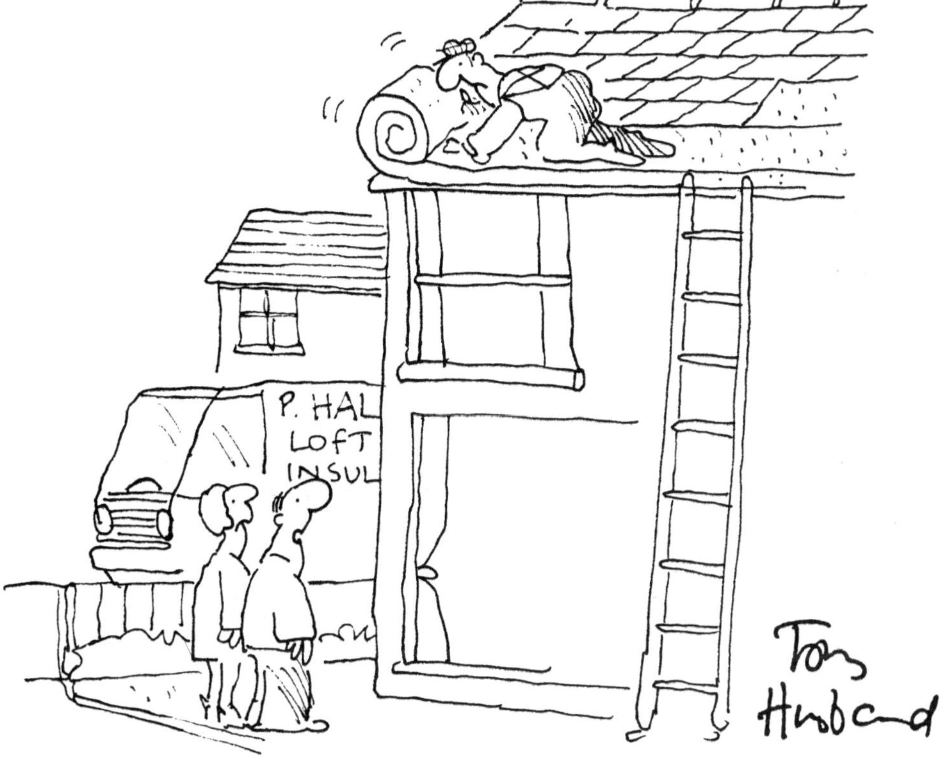
P. HAL
LOFT
INSUL
Tom Husband

*"'Scuse me, shouldn't the insulation be on the inside?"*

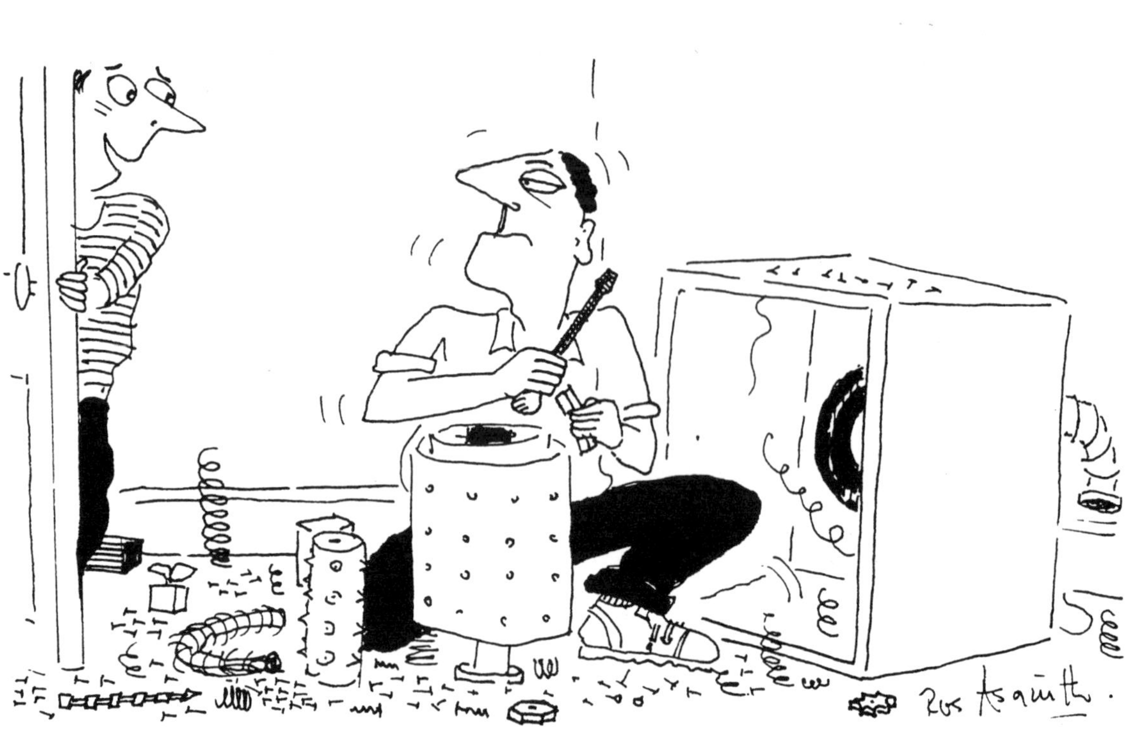
Ros Asquith.

*"Um . . . apparently it was just a power cut . . ."*

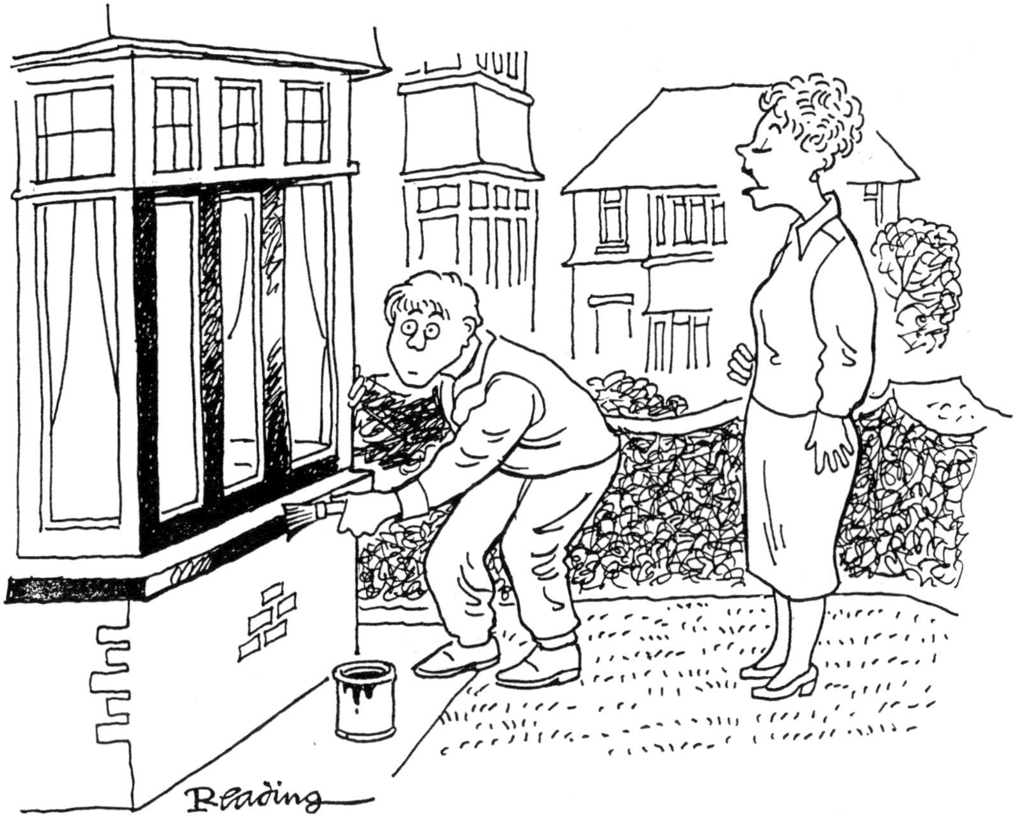
Reading

*"I'm not so sure about the green now that the people next door like it."*

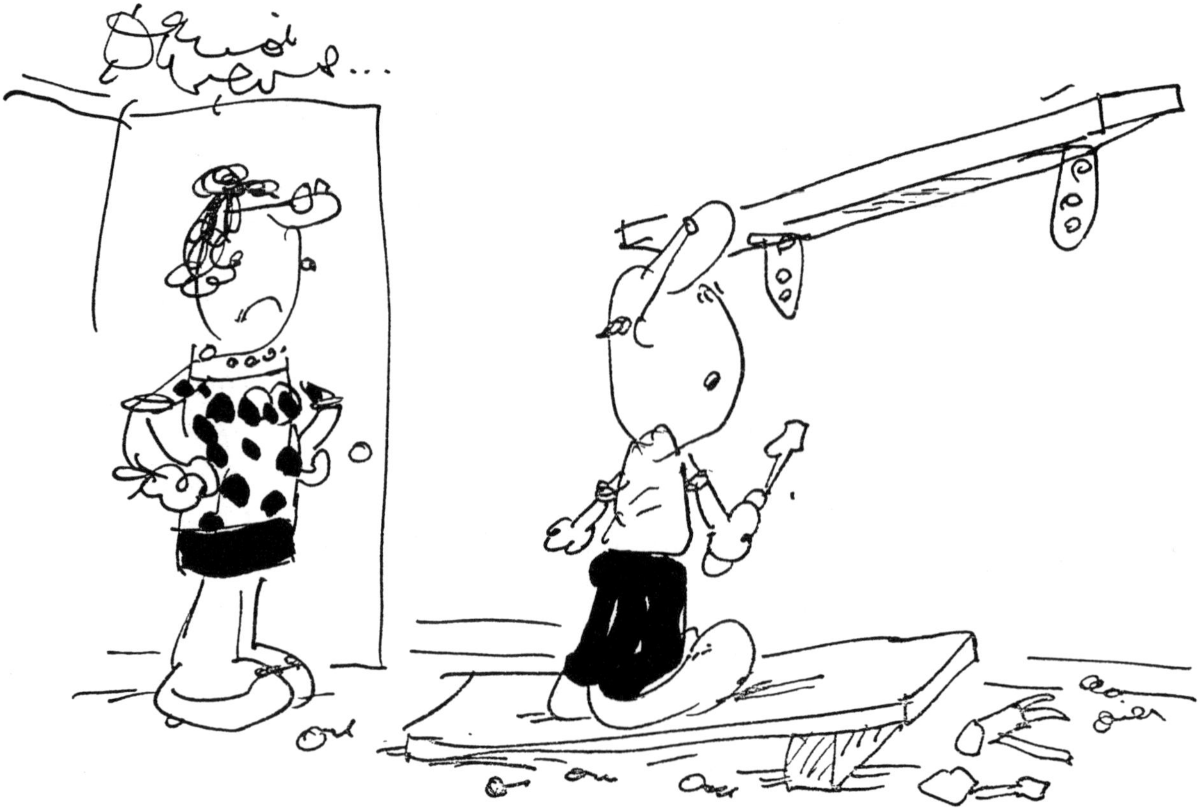

*"Well, it looks just fine to me . . ."*

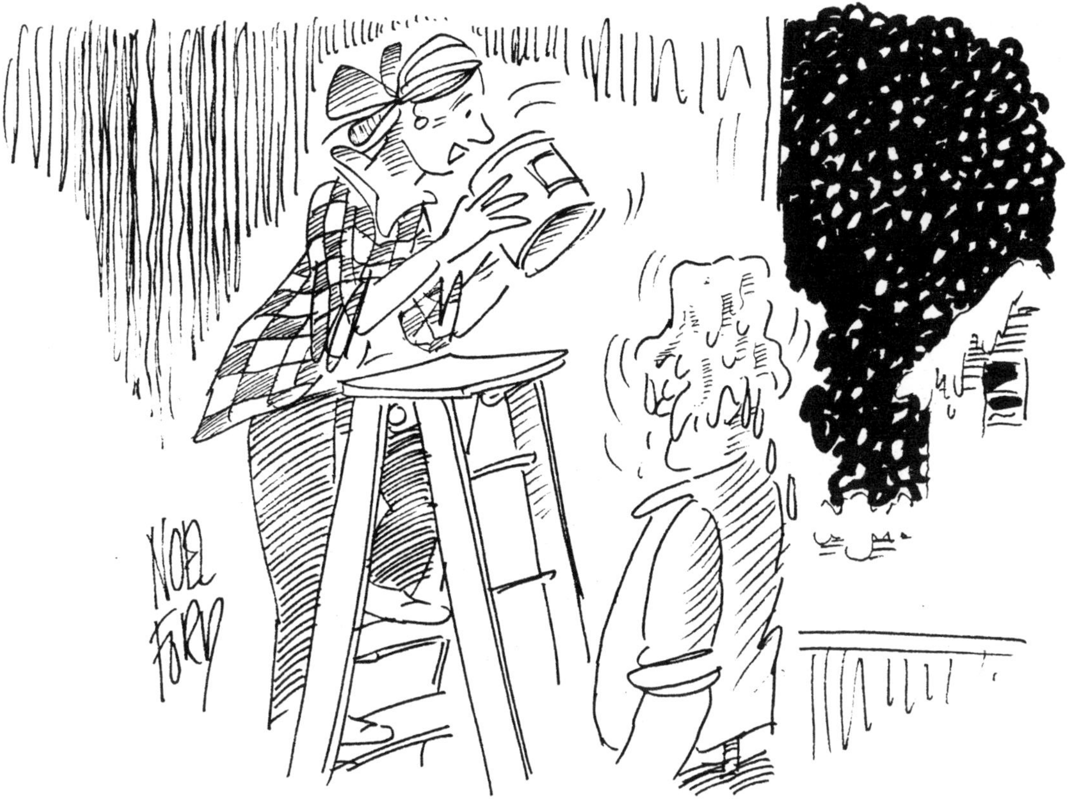
NOEL FORD

"You were right, it wasn't frozen solid, it was just non-drip . . ."

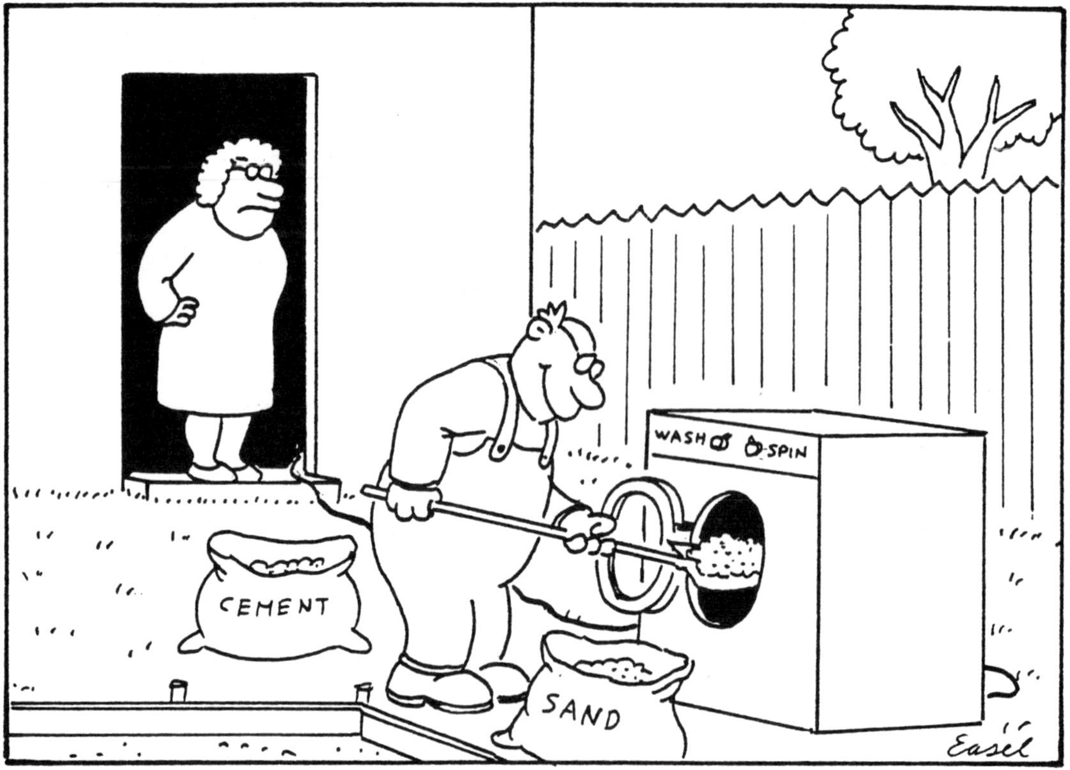
WASH
SPIN
CEMENT
SAND
Easel

*Make-shift concrete mixer.*

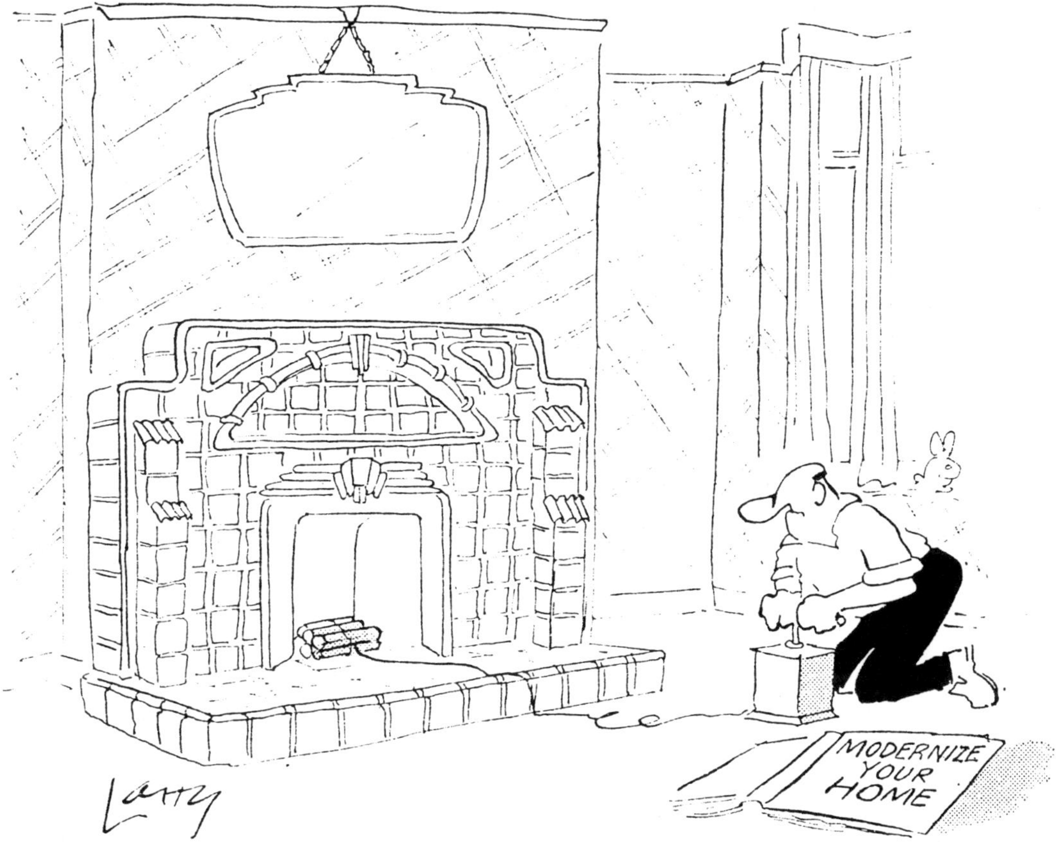
Larry
MODERNIZE
YOUR
HOME

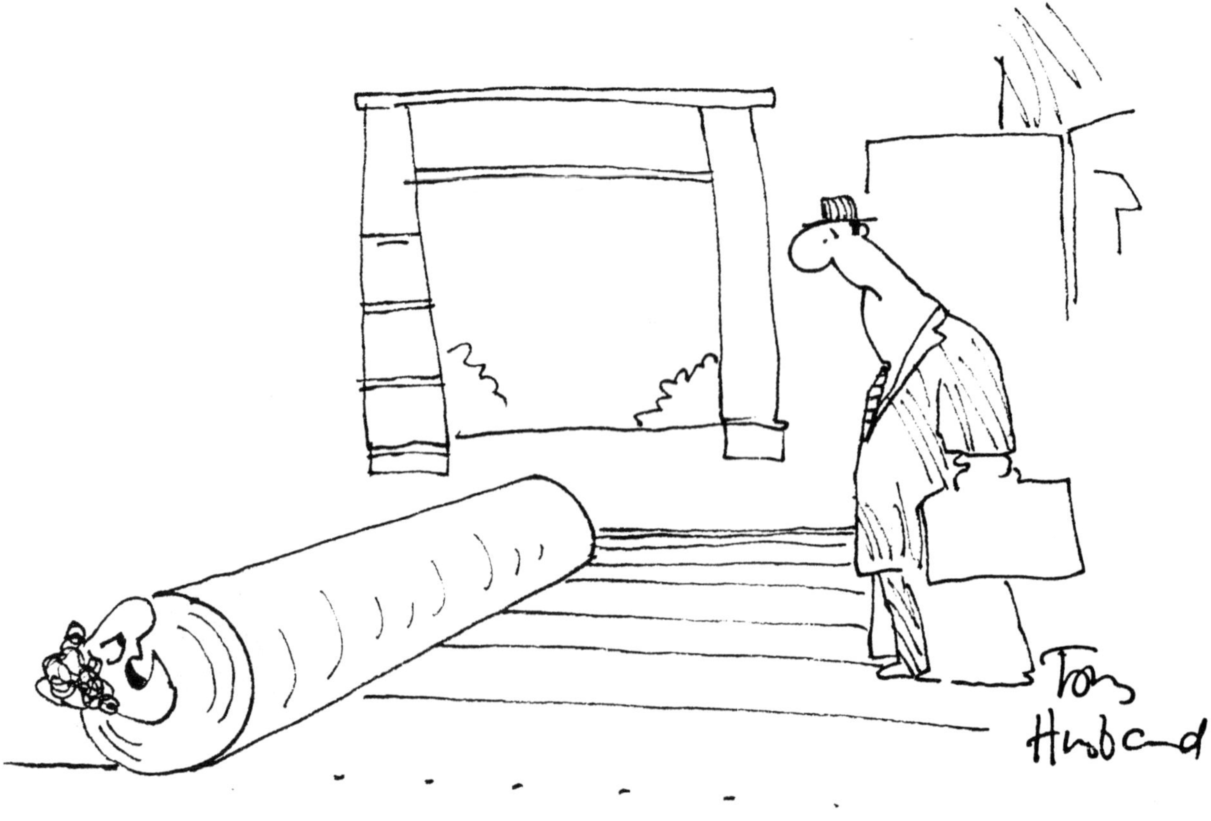
Tony Husband

"You didn't nail the carpet down properly, did you?"

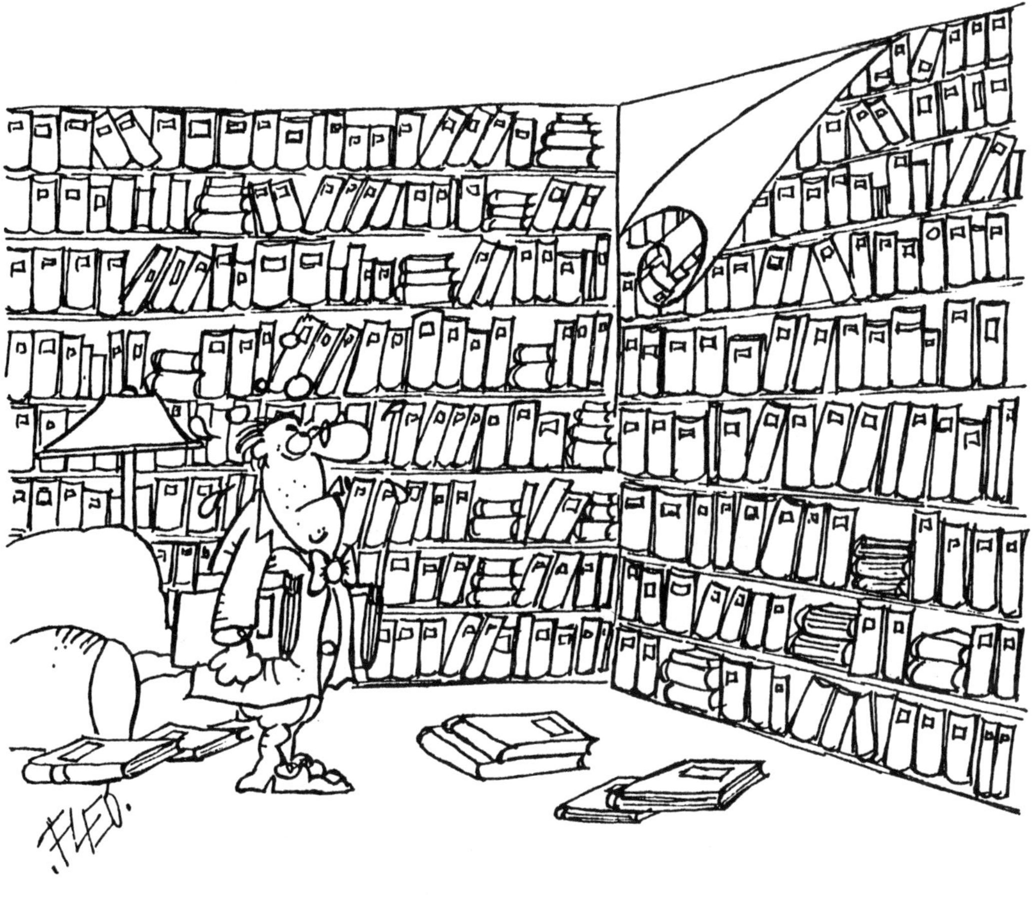

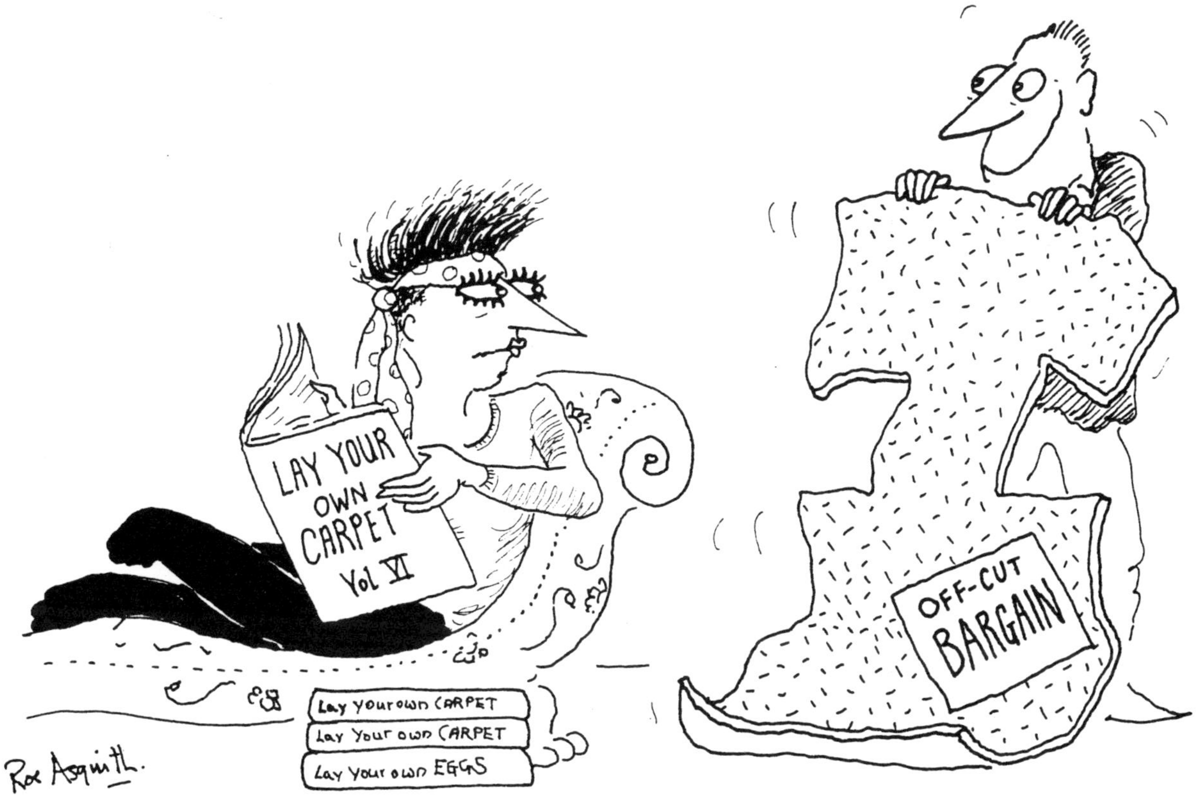
LAY YOUR OWN CARPET Vol VI
OFF-CUT BARGAIN
Lay your own CARPET
Lay Your own CARPET
Lay Your own EGGS
Ros Asquith.

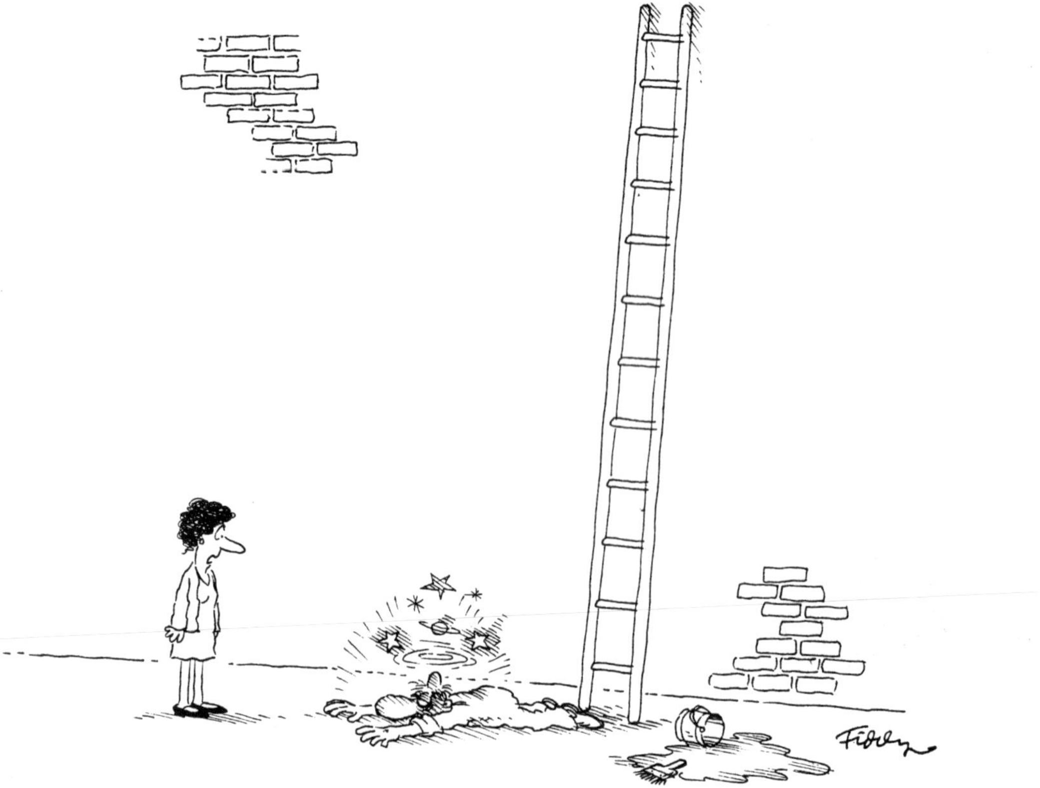

*"You should go up again immediately or you'll lose your nerve!"*

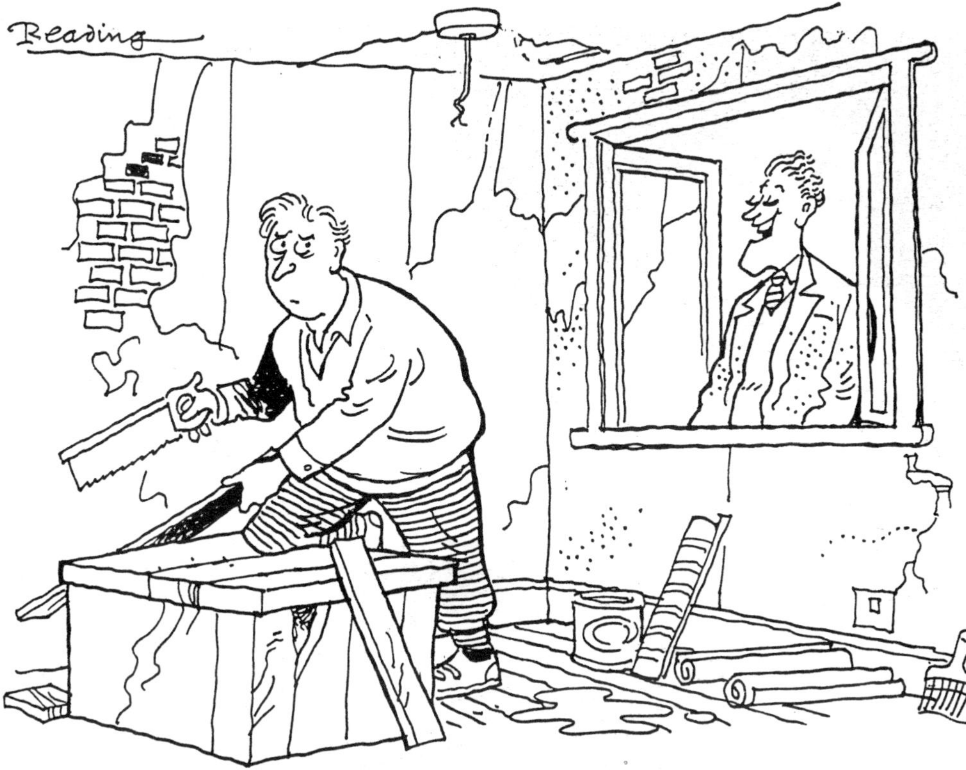
Reading

*"I'm from a do-it-yourself magazine, and we're doing an article on the most common mistakes . . ."*

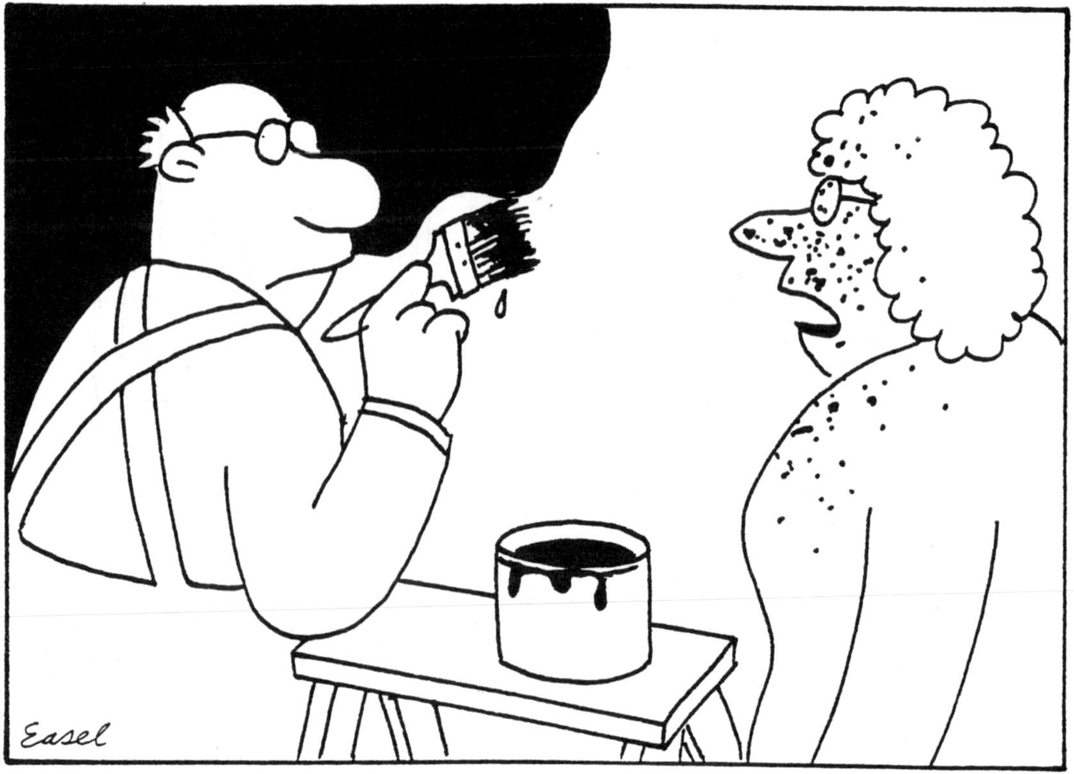
Easel

"Bless you."

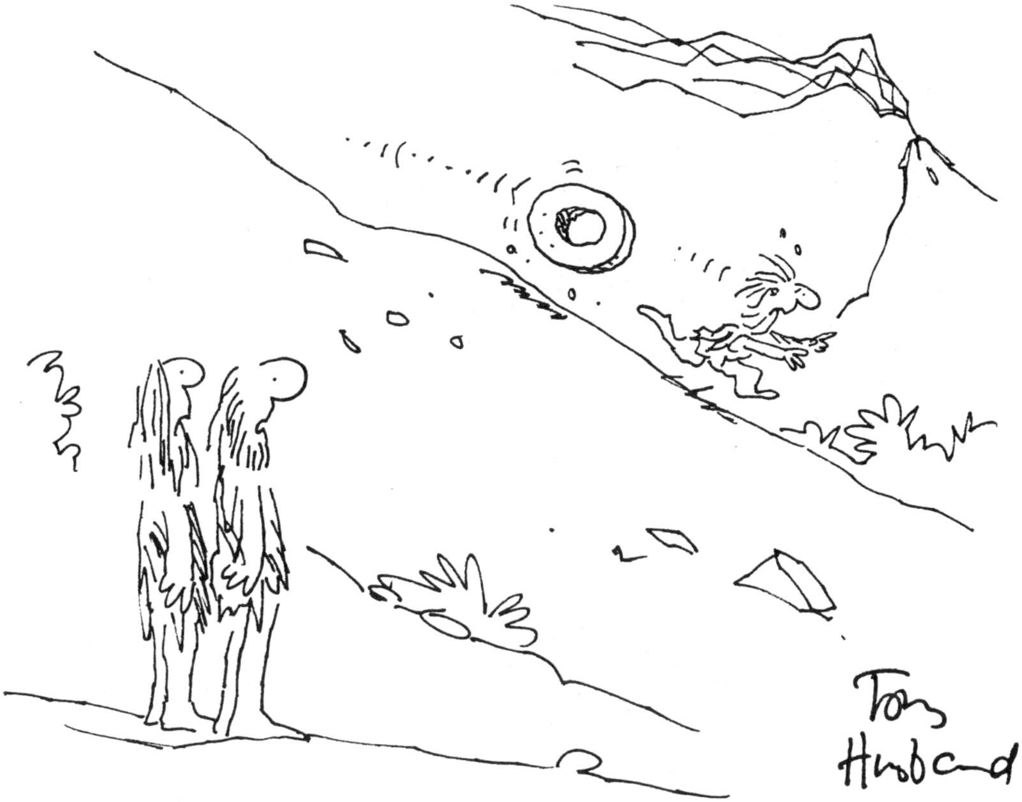
Tom Husband

*"Hello, what's he invented this time?"*

*"Mrs Fossett's husband put his back out half-way <u>through</u> the decorating, but y<u>ou</u> have to do it carrying the <u>pattern books</u> home!"*

*"He invented the first do-it-yourself kit for kitchen shelves."*

21

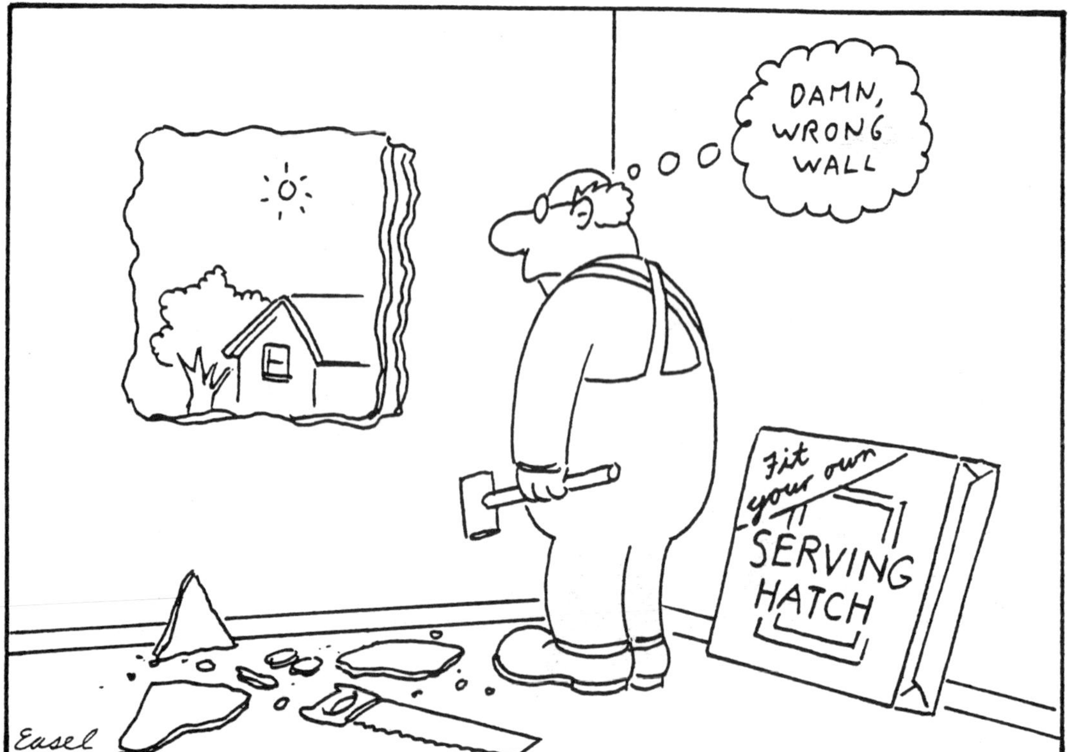
DAMN, WRONG WALL
Fit your own
SERVING HATCH
Easel

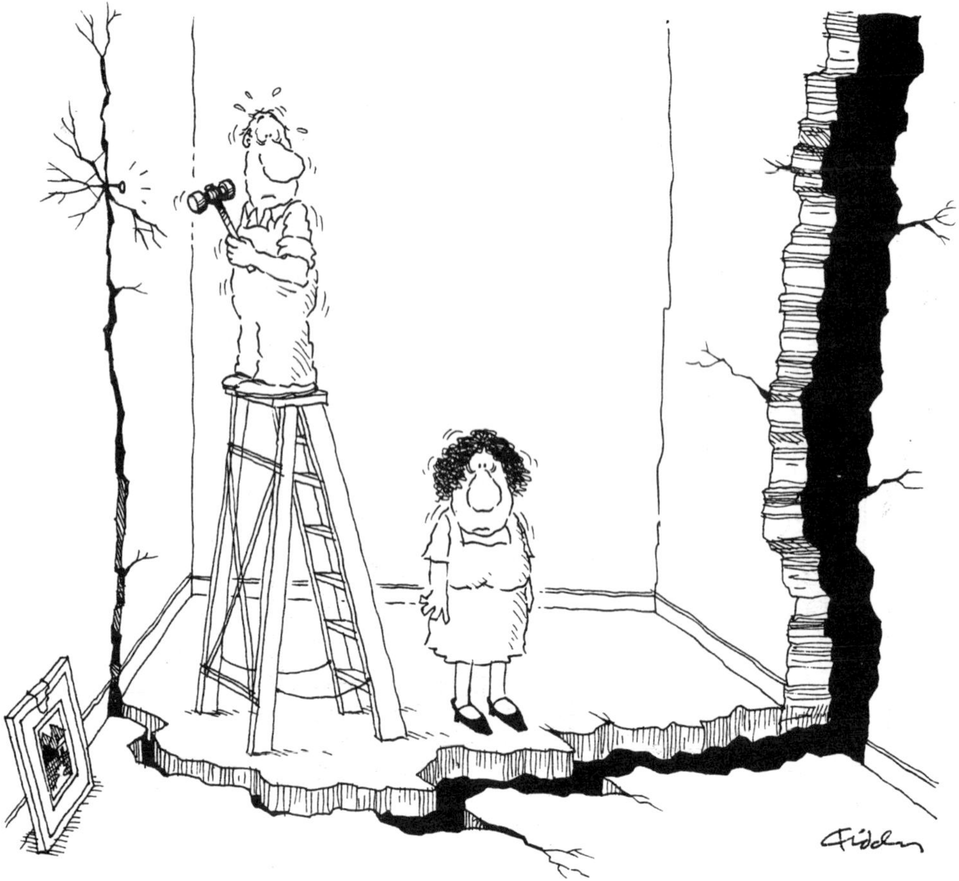

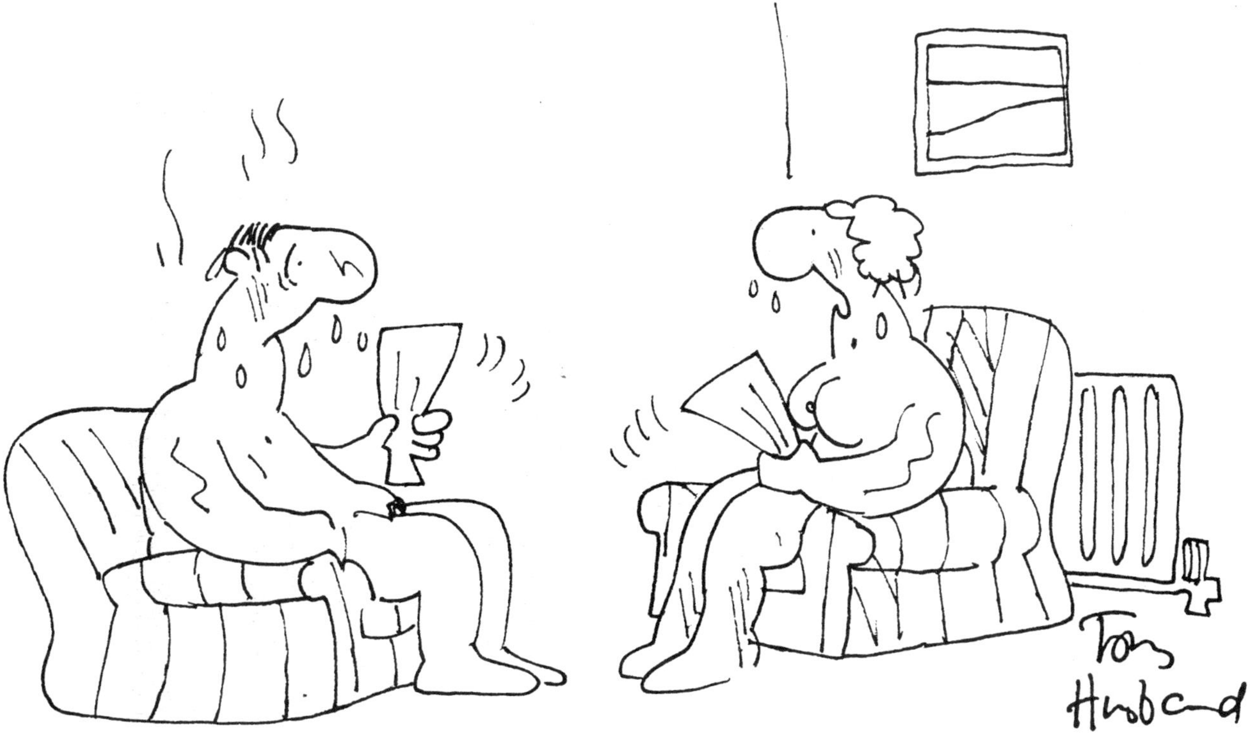
Tony
Husband

*"Next time the central heating breaks down, leave it alone and hire an expert."*

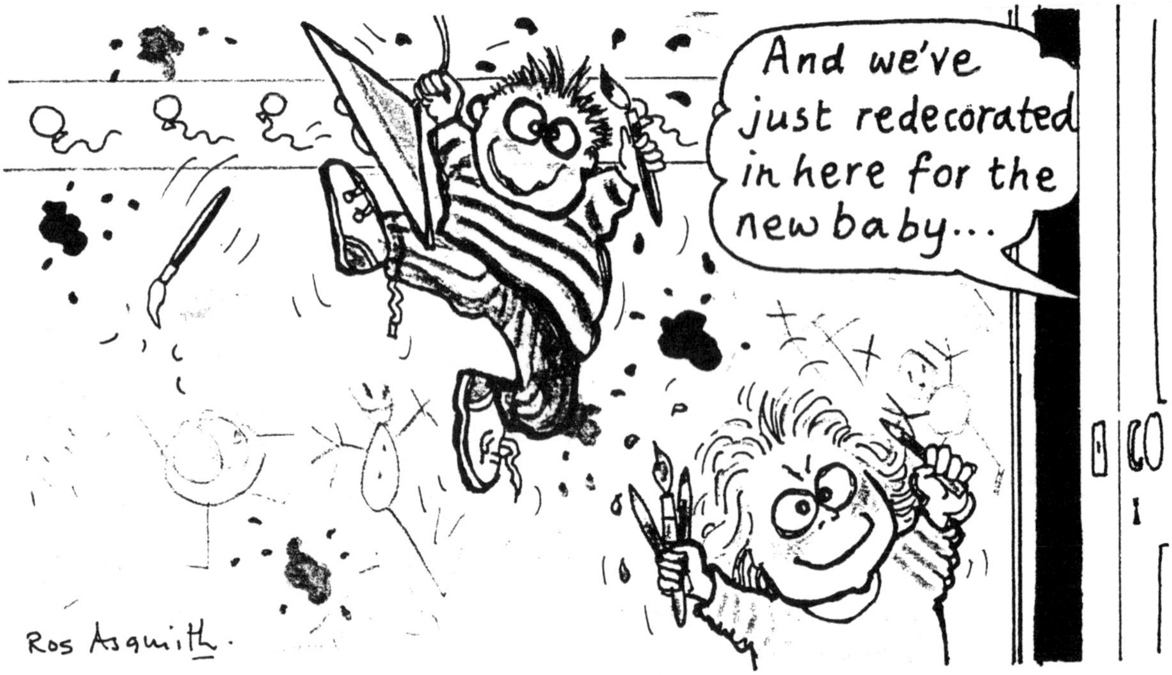
And we've just redecorated in here for the new baby...
Ros Asquith.

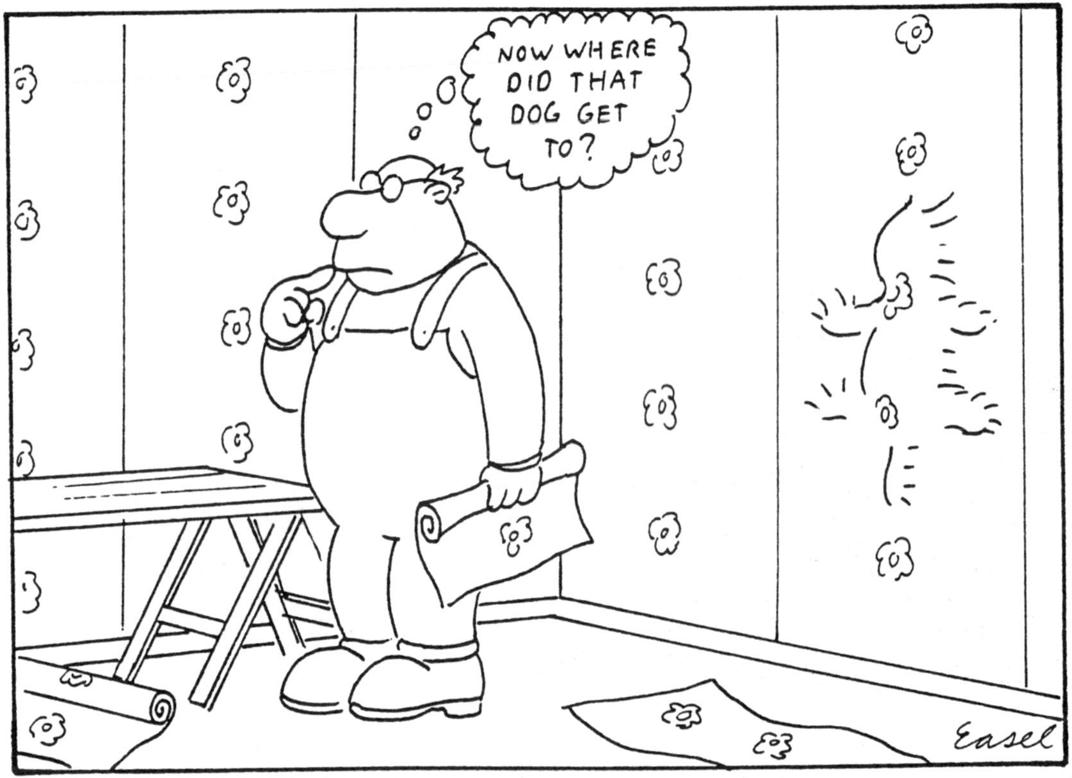
NOW WHERE DID THAT DOG GET TO?
Easel

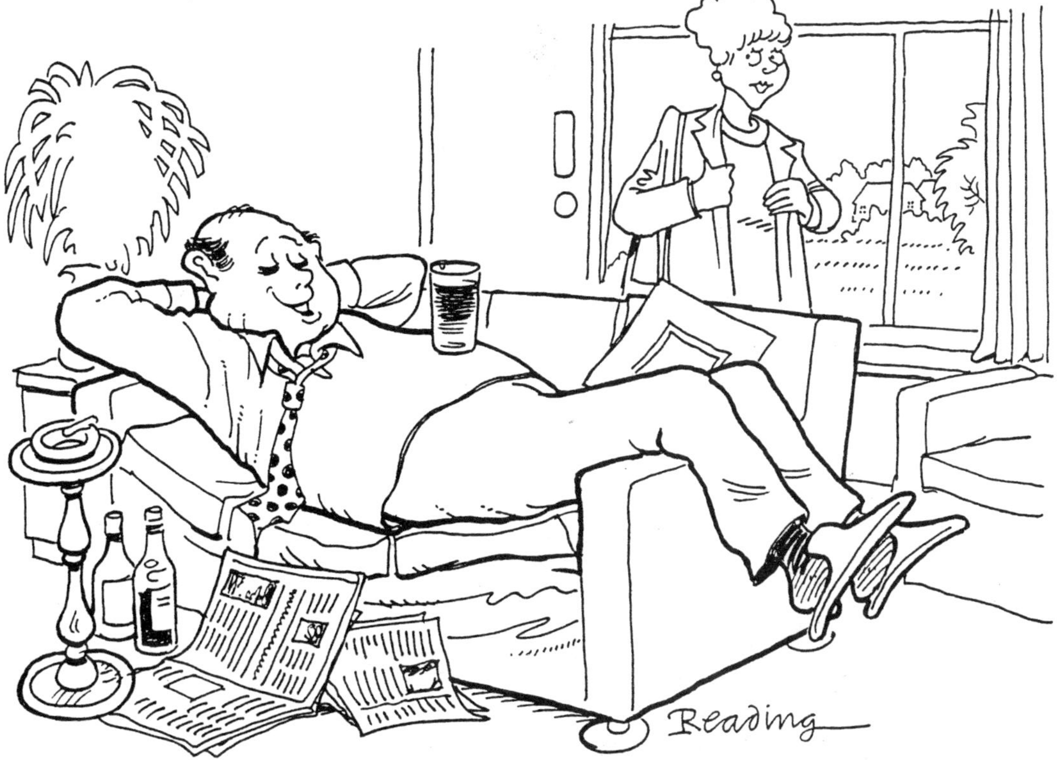
Reading

*"I <u>know</u> a do-it-yourself craze is sweeping the country, but some of us have to keep our heads."*

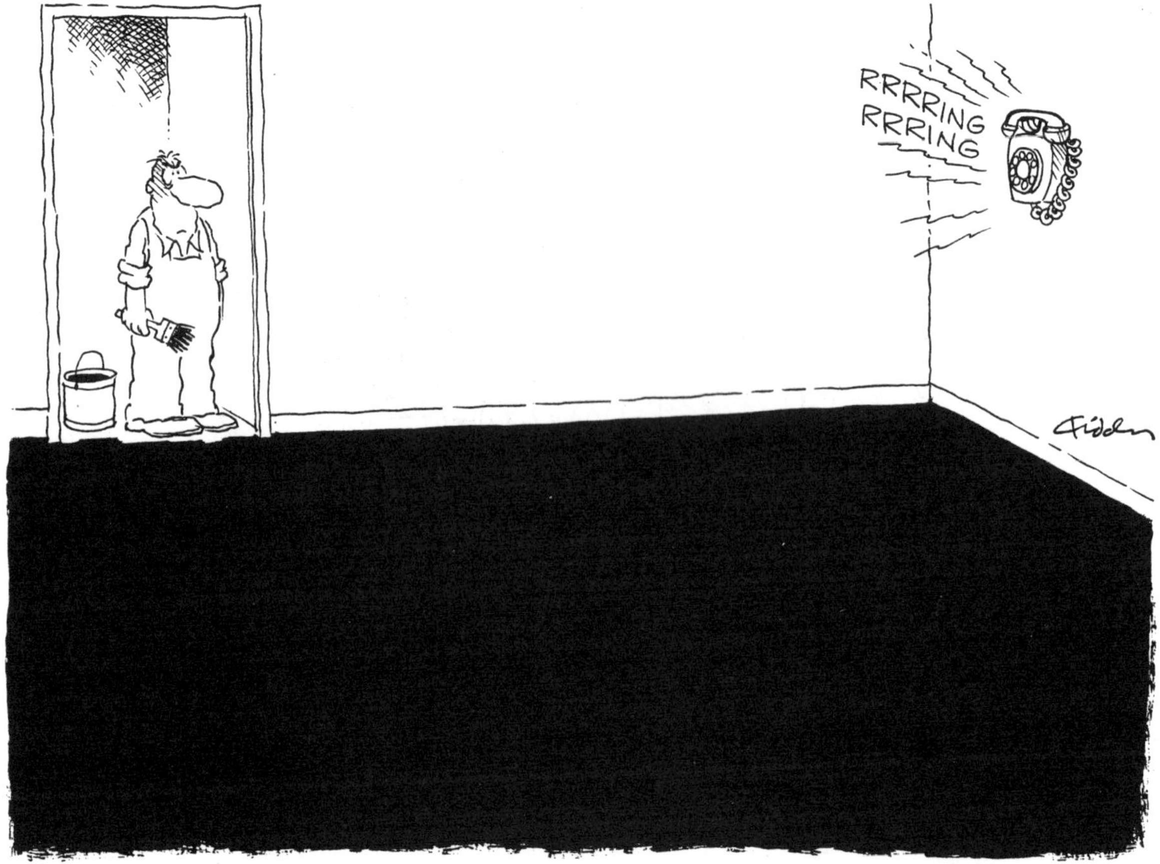
RRRRING
RRRING

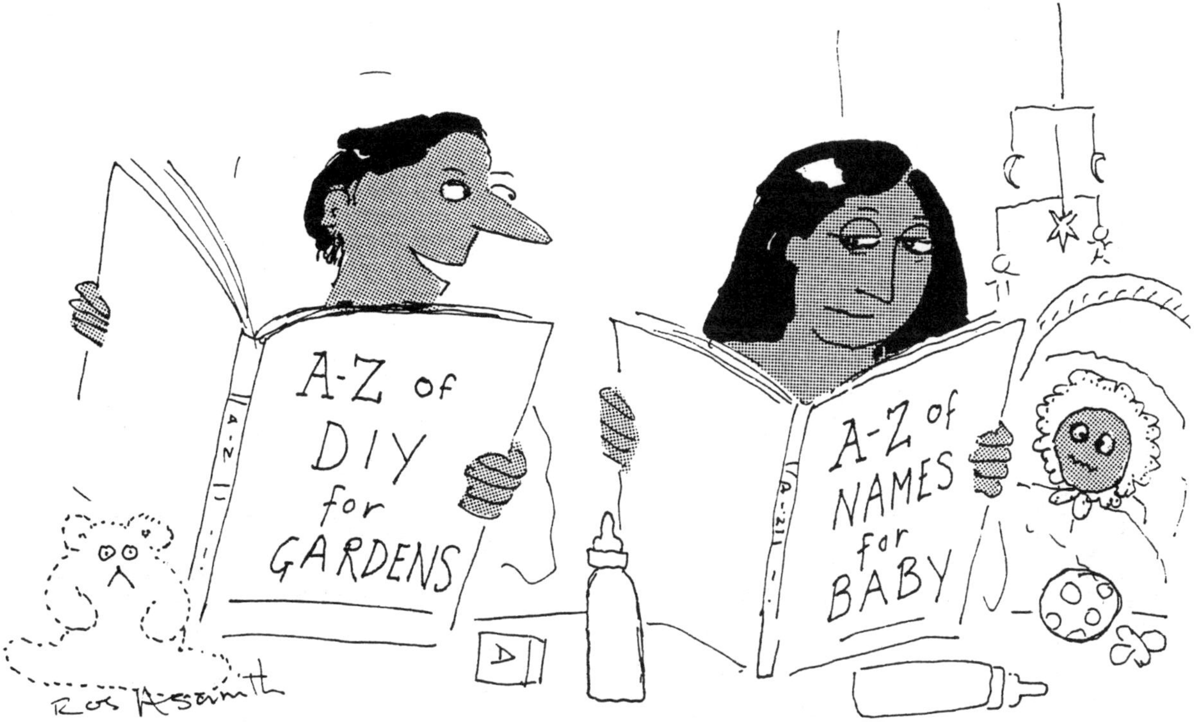
A-Z of DIY for GARDENS
A-Z of NAMES for BABY
D

*"Why don't we name her Pergola?"*

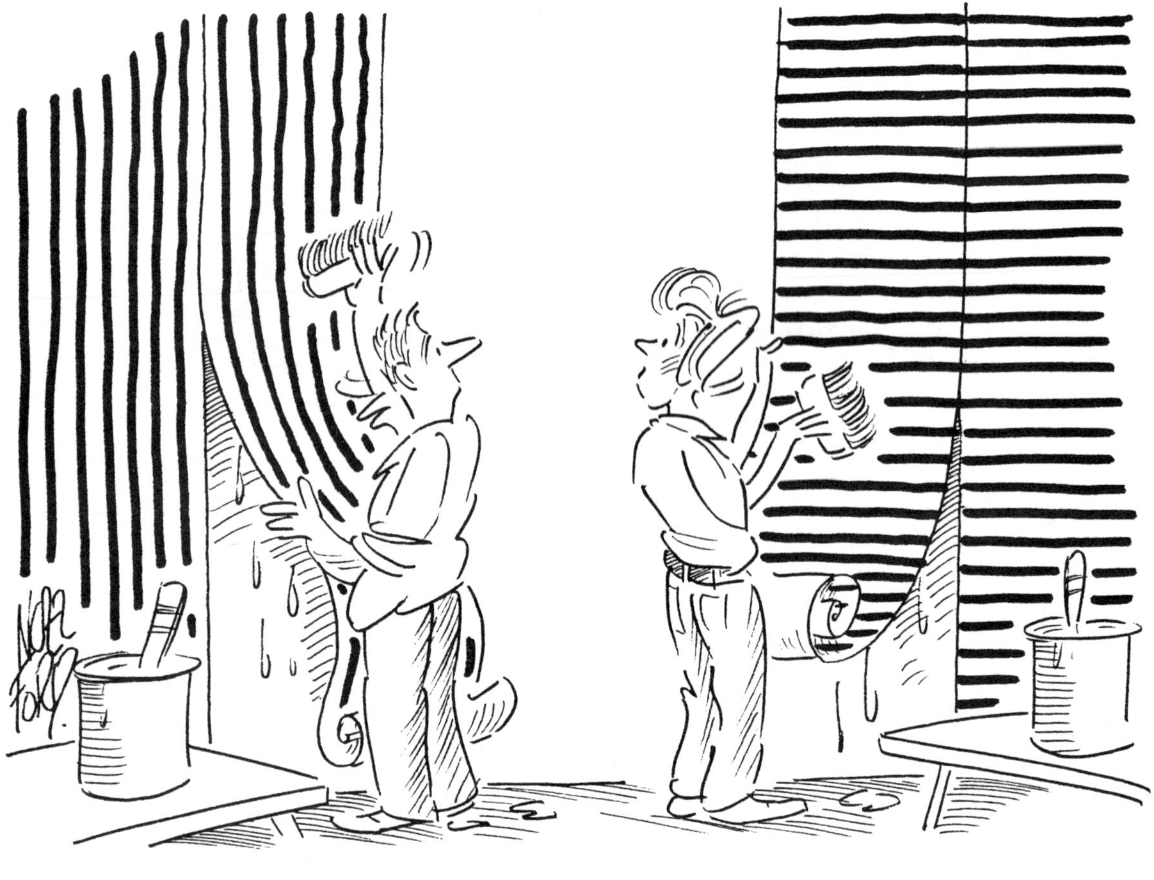

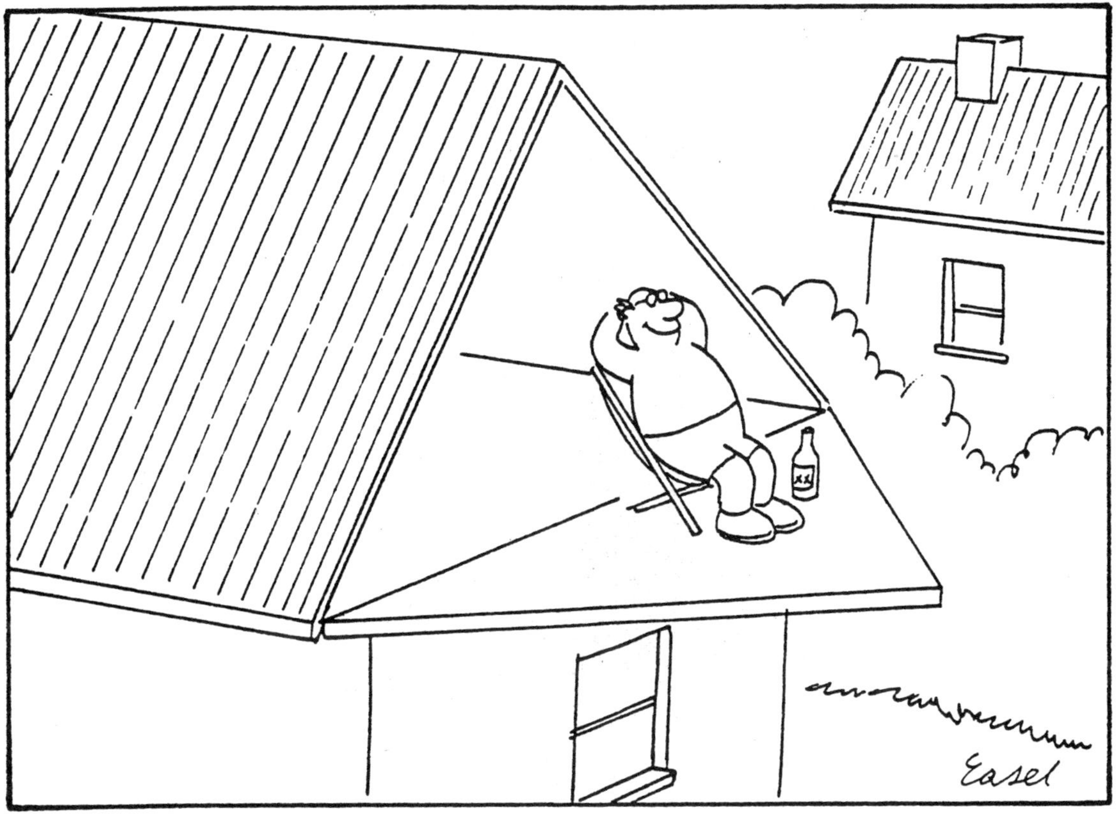
Easel

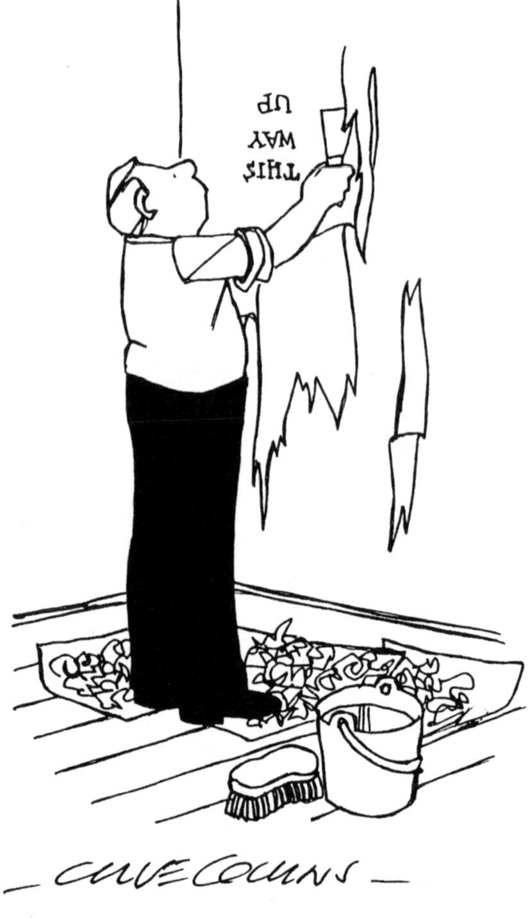
THIS WAY UP
CLIVE COLLINS

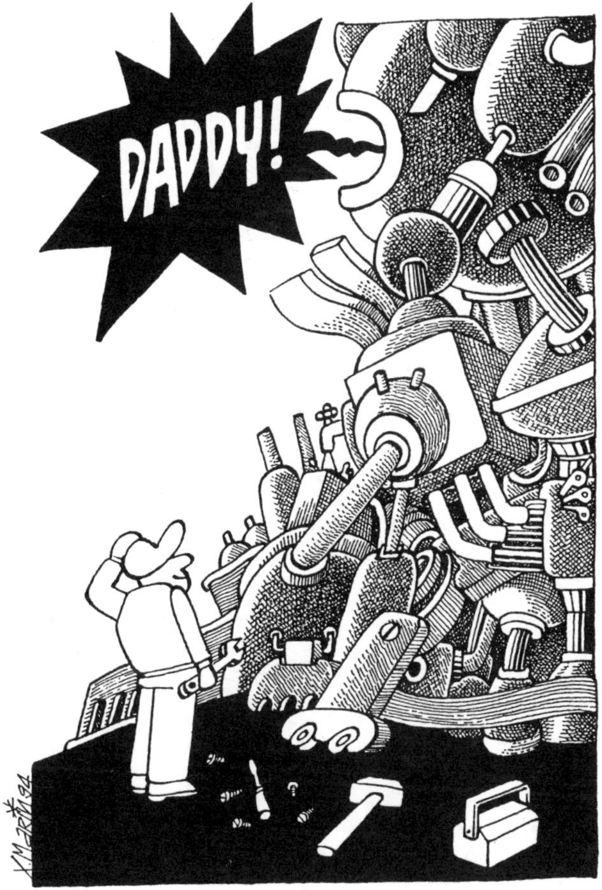
DADDY!

*"I'm looking for a nice tasteful emulsion to blend in with yellow carpet, purple furnishings and green-and-red-striped curtains."*

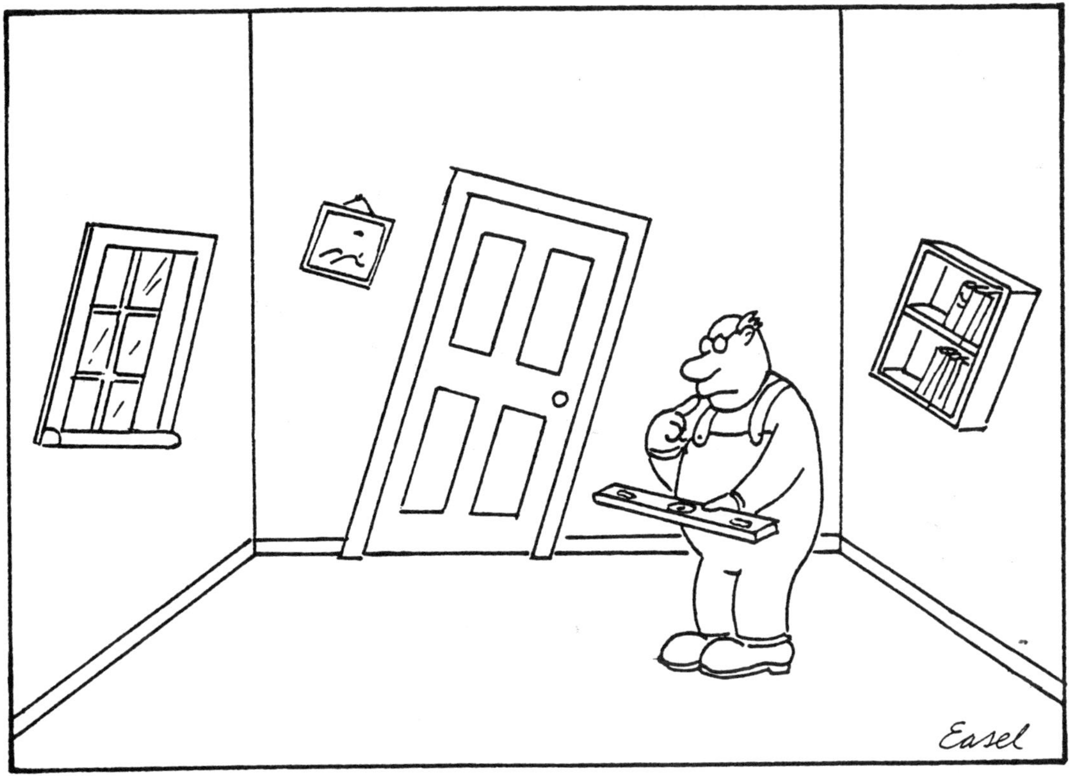
Easel

*Stan finally realized that his spirit-level was defective.*

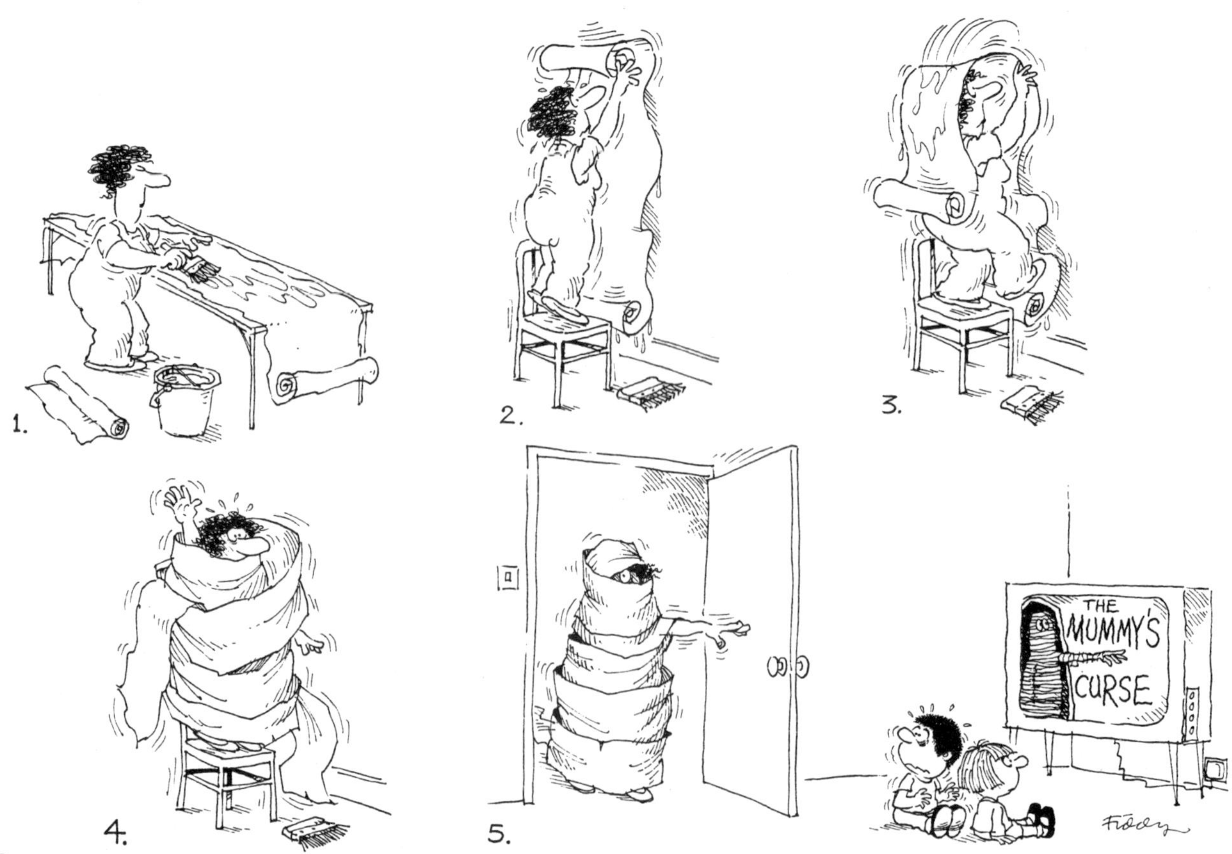
1.
2.
3.
4.
5.
THE MUMMY'S CURSE

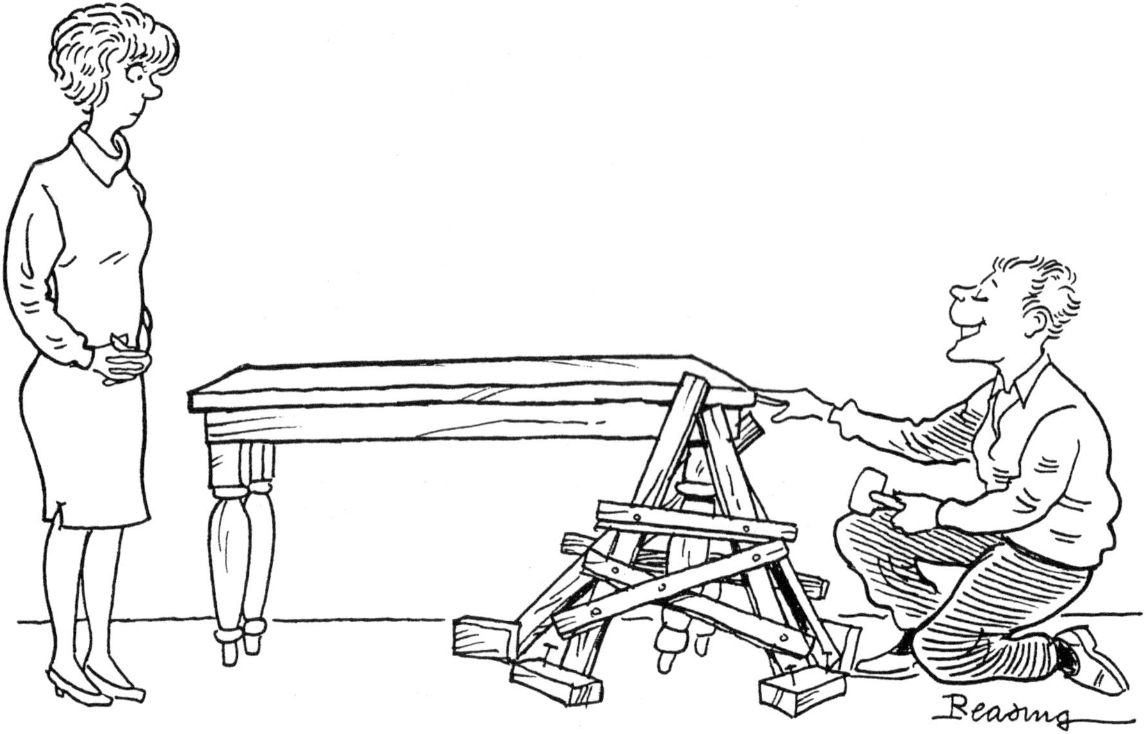
Reading

*"That should hold it for a while."*

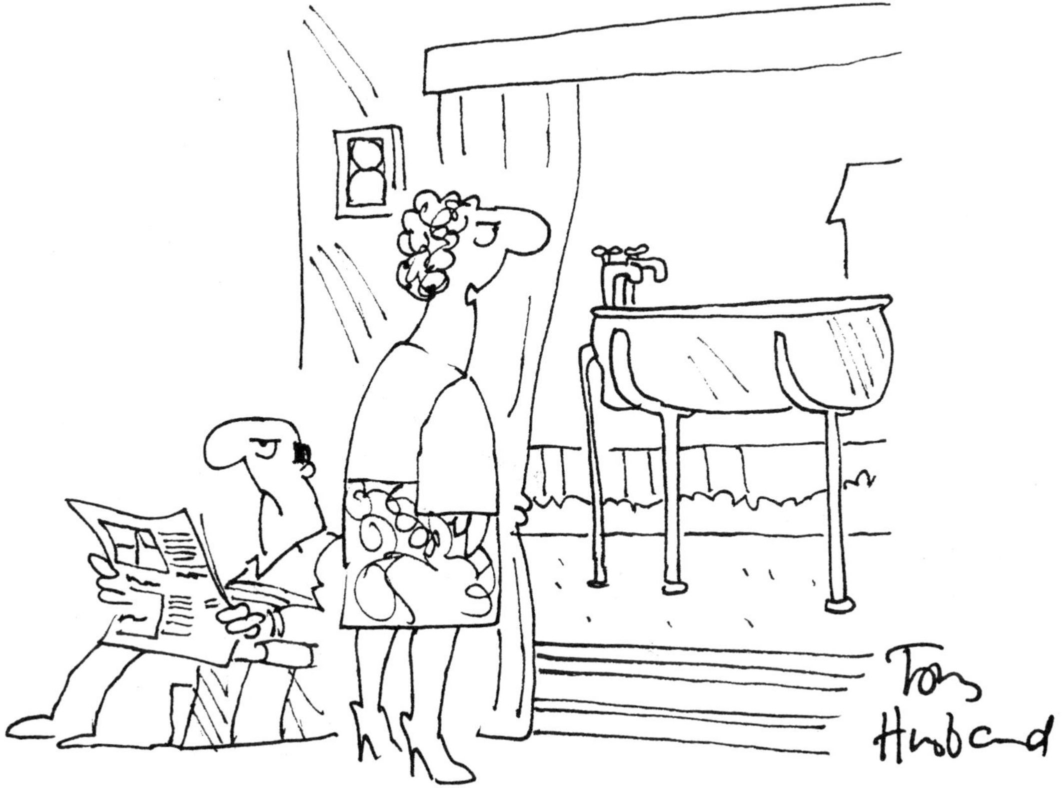
Tom Hubbard

*"Actually, it's not the sort of bird-bath I had in mind."*

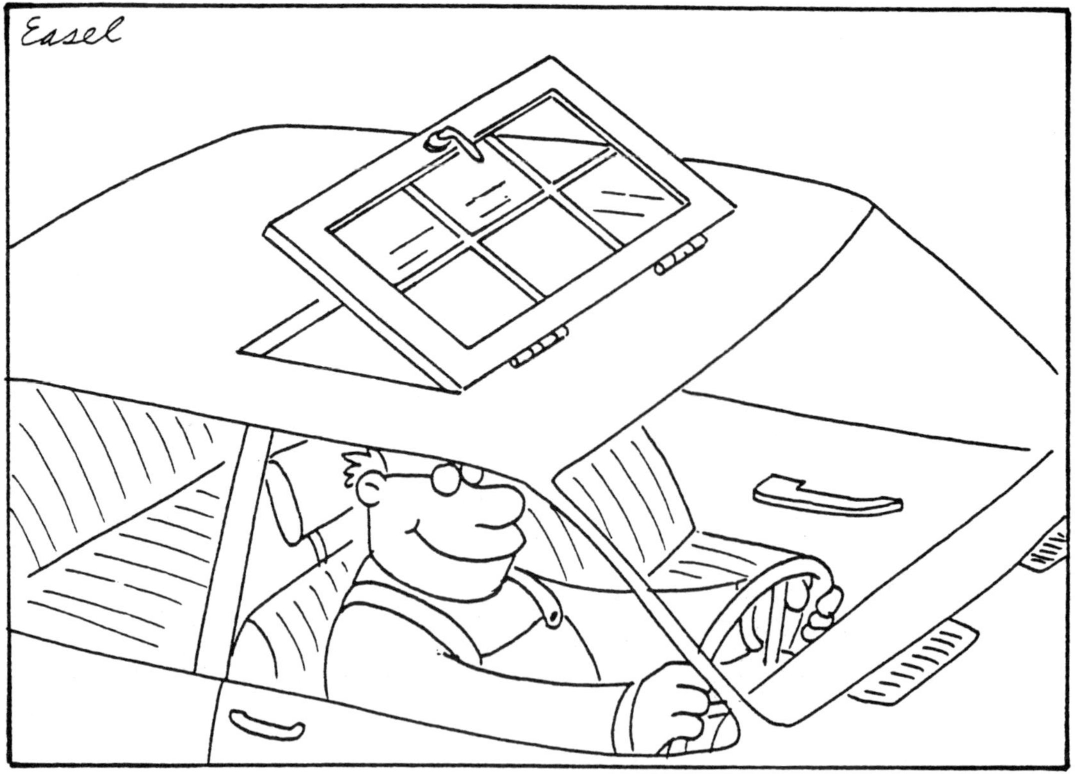
Easel

*Poor man's sunroof.*

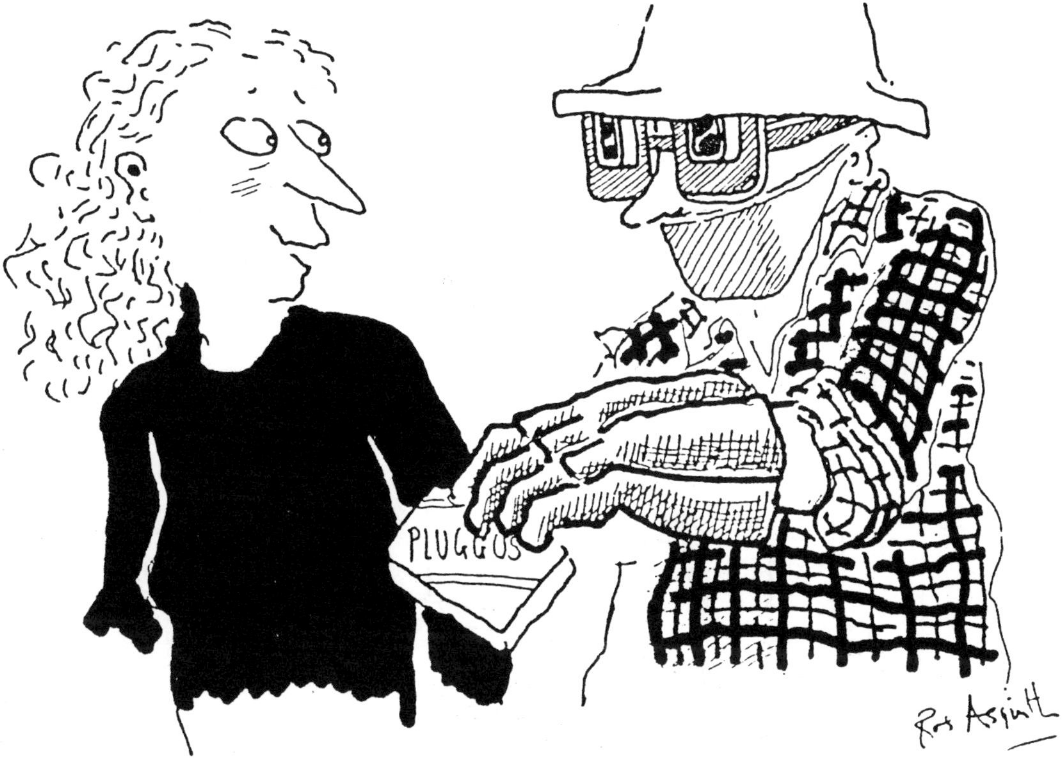
PLUGGOS
Ros Asquith

*"Do you really need earplugs just to hang a picture?"*

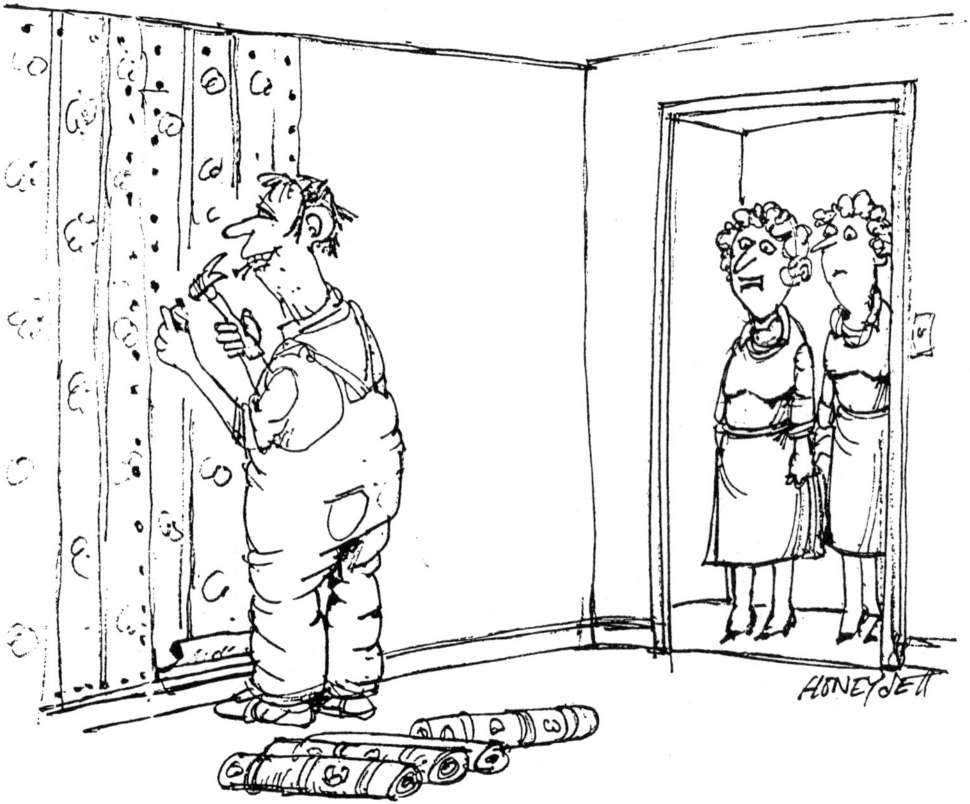

"As well as being cheap, he's also very quick."

A
B
KENJI

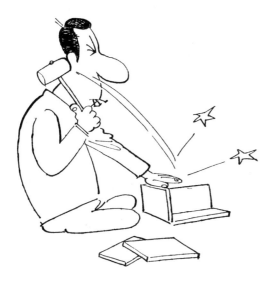

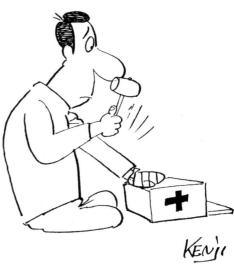

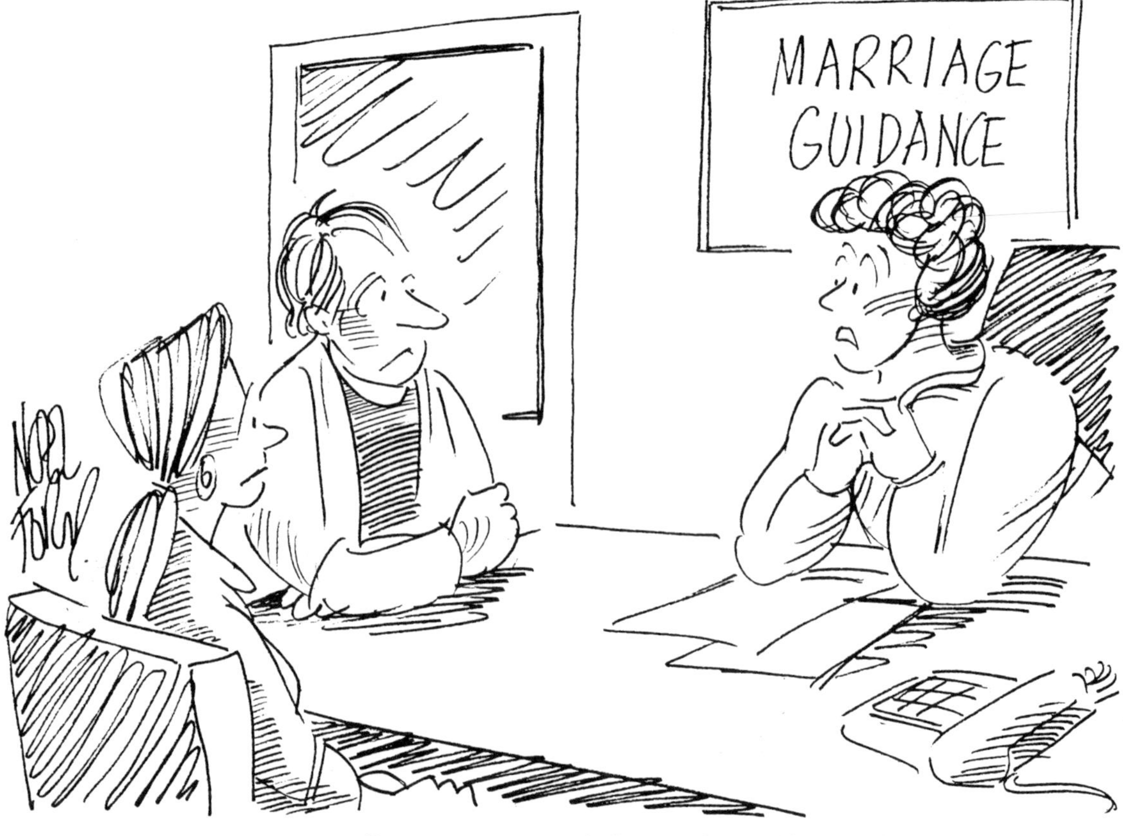
MARRIAGE
GUIDANCE

*"I'm sorry – I really can't come and choose the wallpaper for you."*

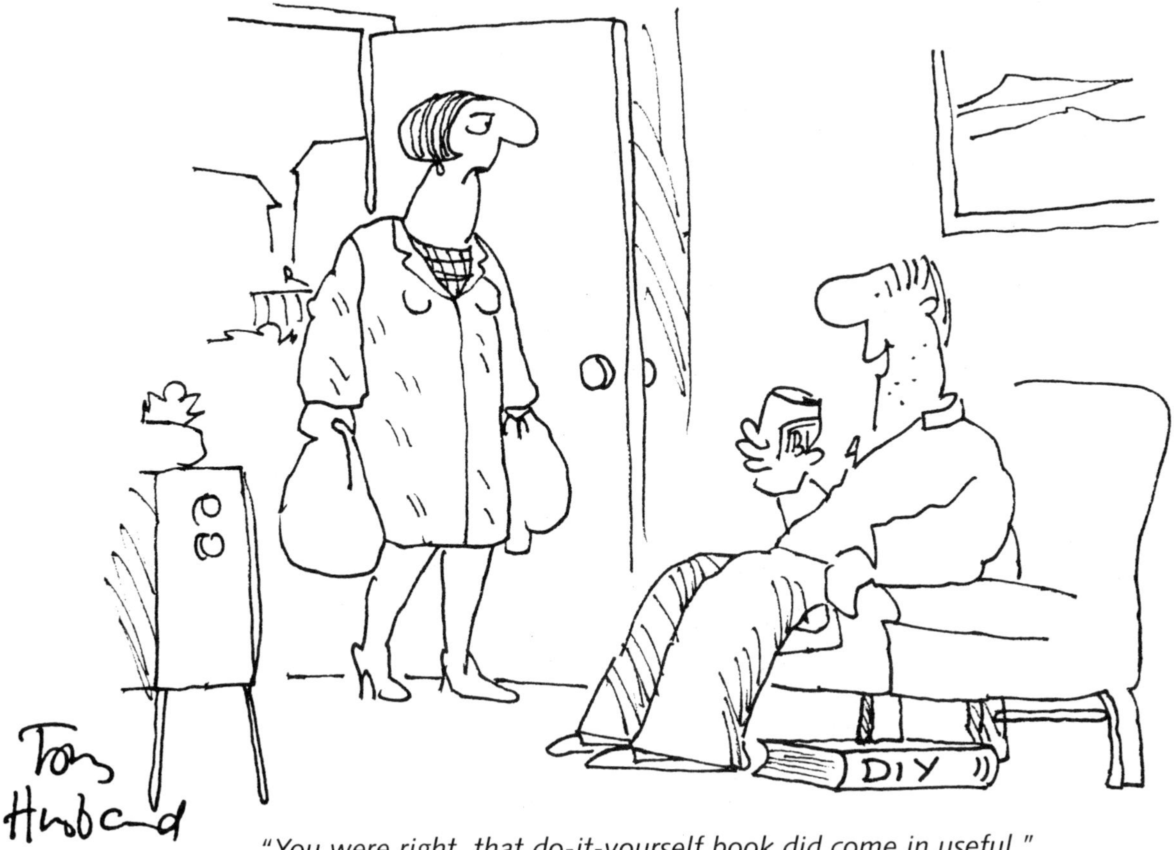
DIY

*"You were right, that do-it-yourself book did come in useful."*

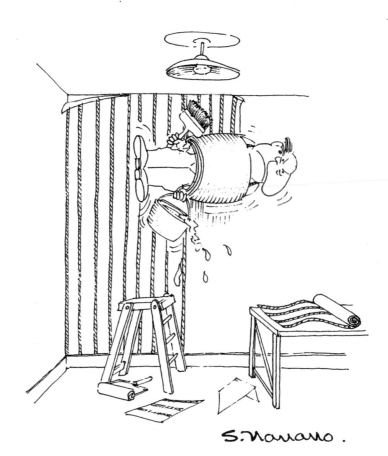

S. Navarro.

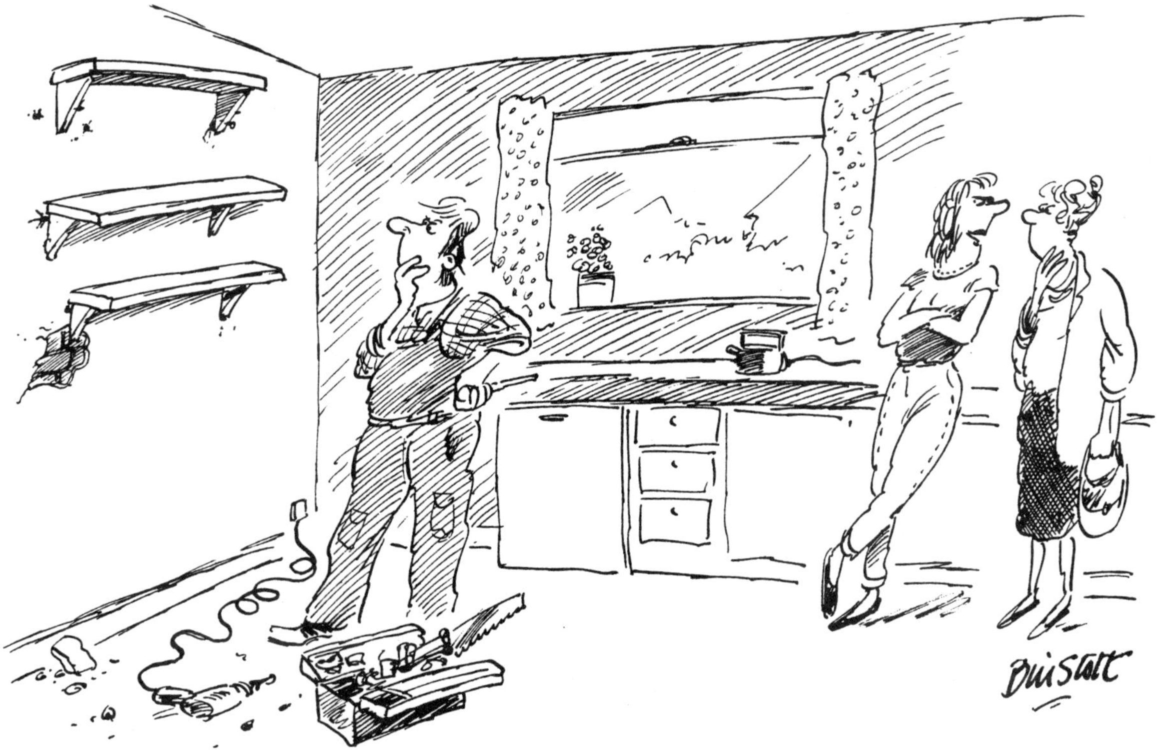
Bill Stott

*"He thinks I love him for his come-to-bed eyes.*
*Actually I'm crazy about the way he can't put shelves up."*

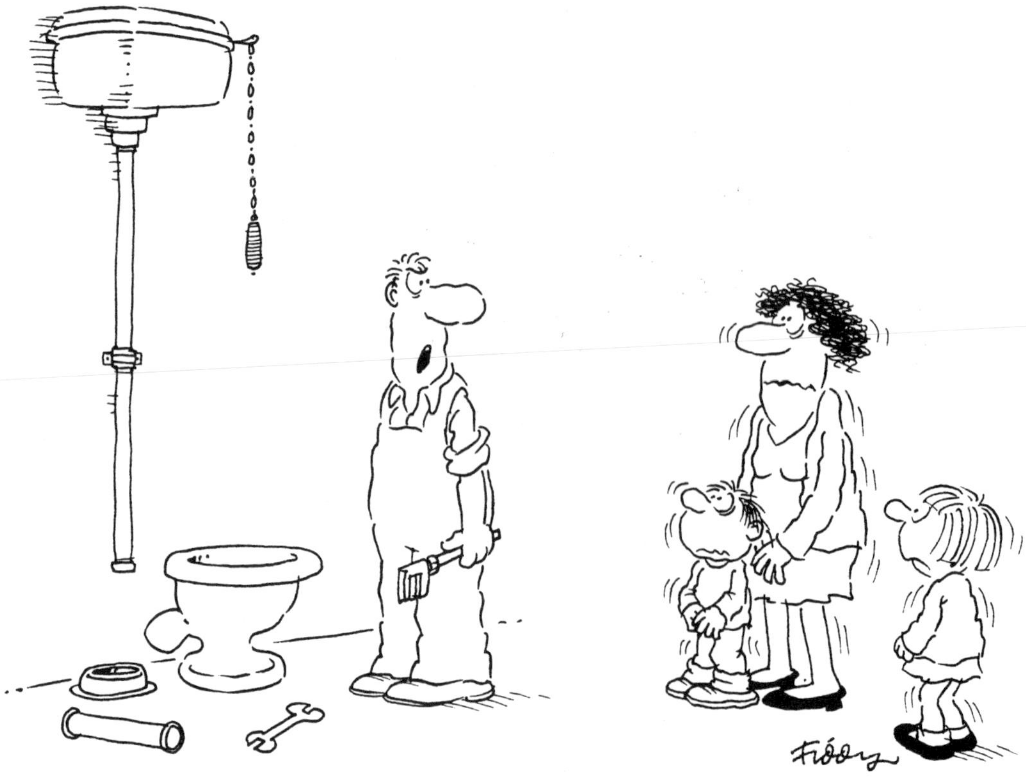

"Don't hurry me! A rushed job is a botched job."

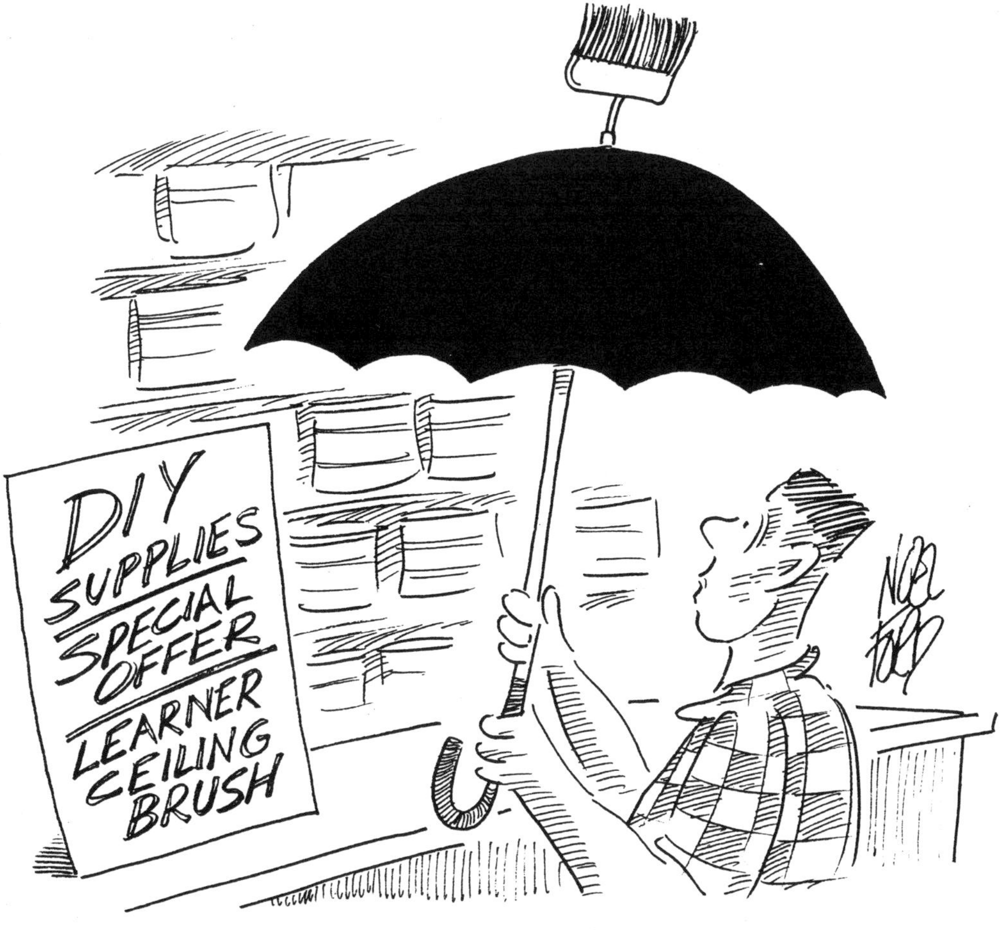
DIY
SUPPLIES
SPECIAL
OFFER
LEARNER
CEILING
BRUSH

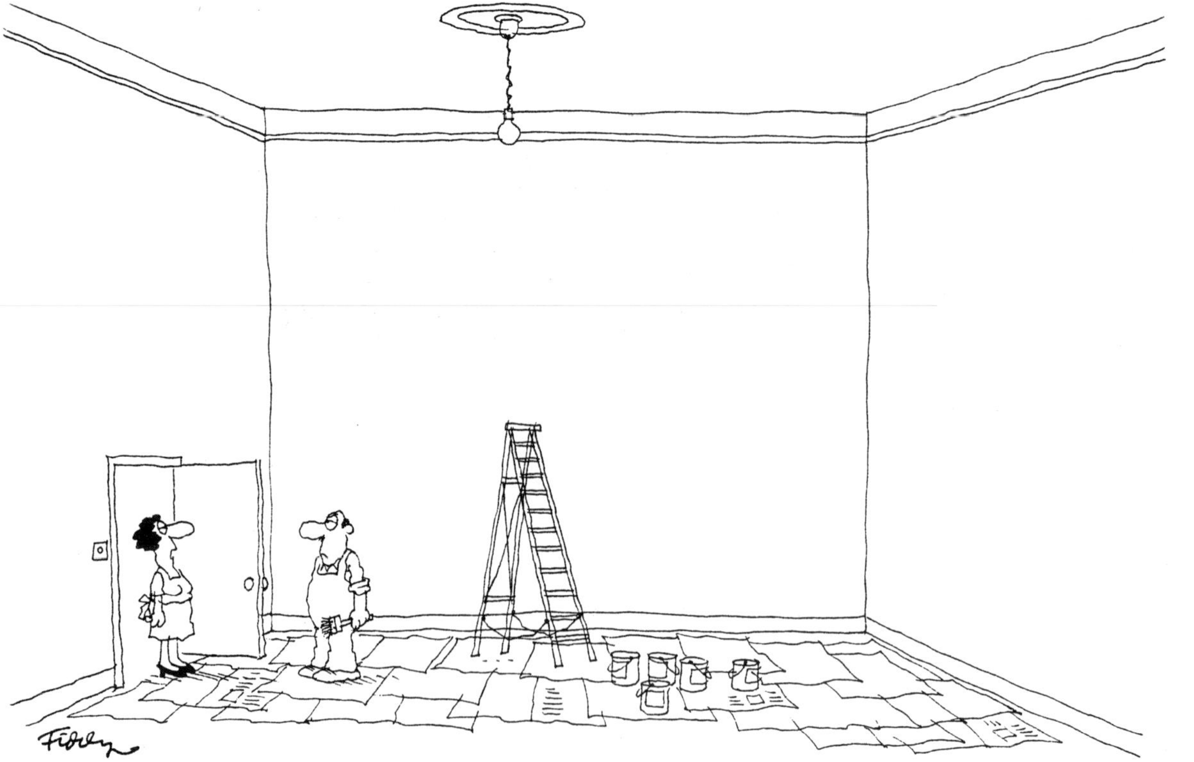
Fibbey

*"I like it, except I <u>hate</u> green!"*

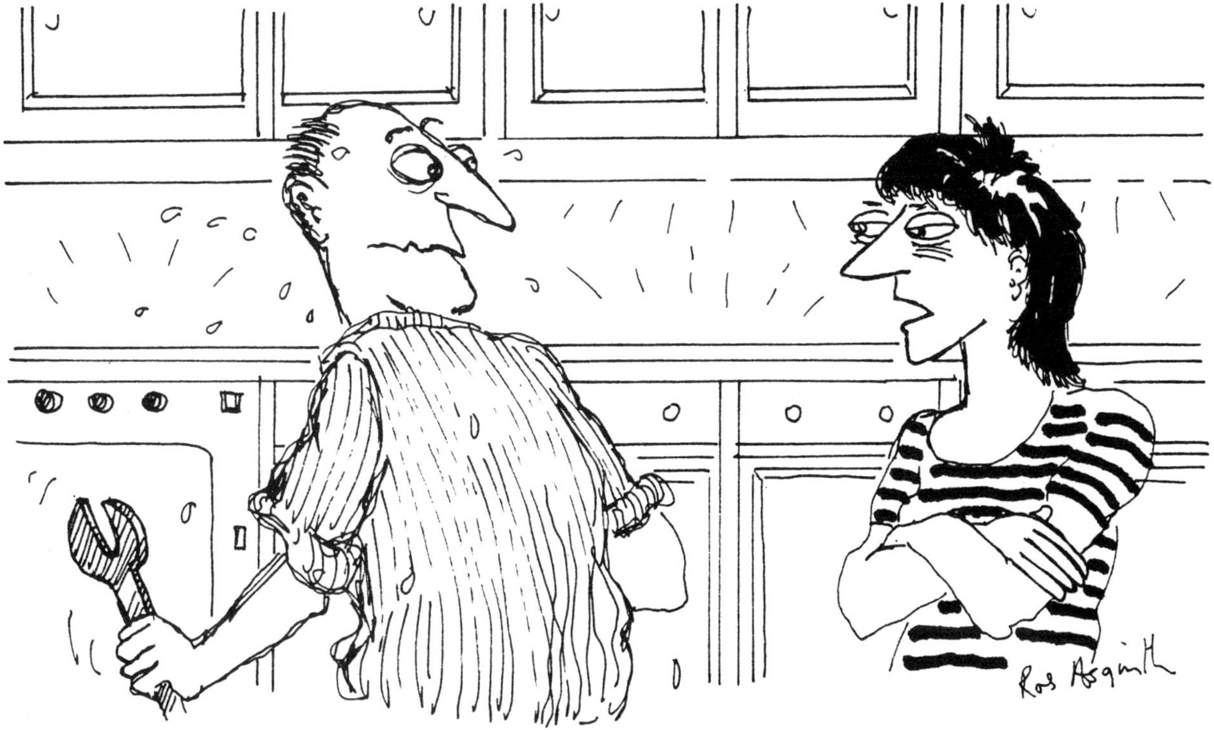

*"Unfortunately, you've put in everything but the kitchen sink."*

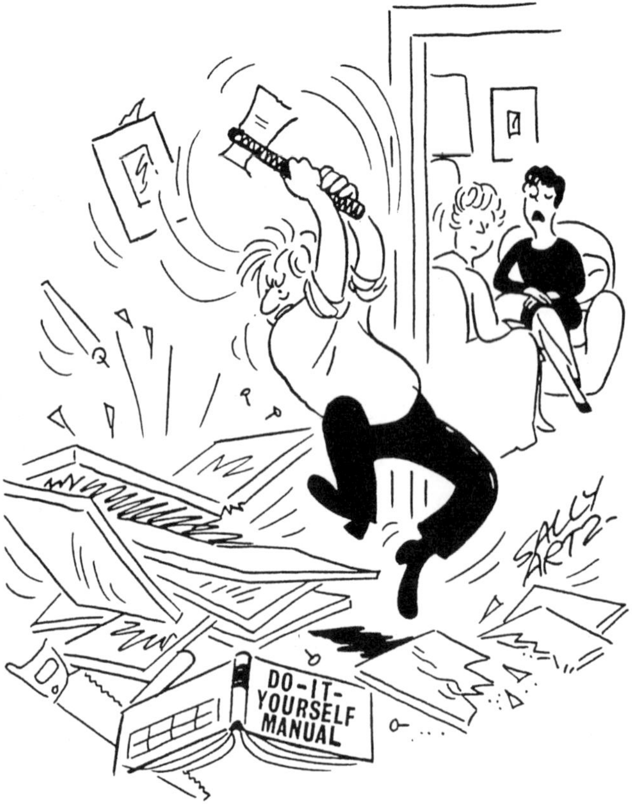
DO-IT-
YOURSELF
MANUAL
SALLY
ARTZ

*"It's only Jim, coming to terms with failure."*

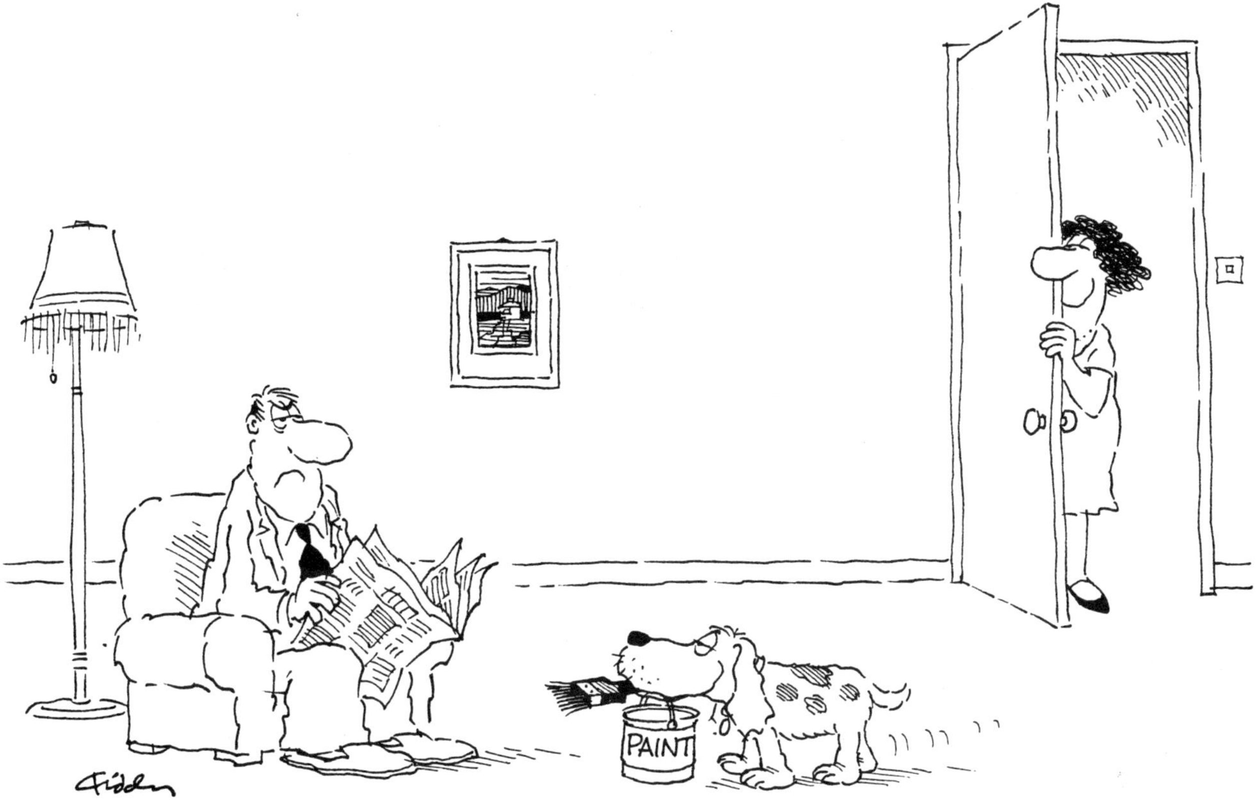
PAINT

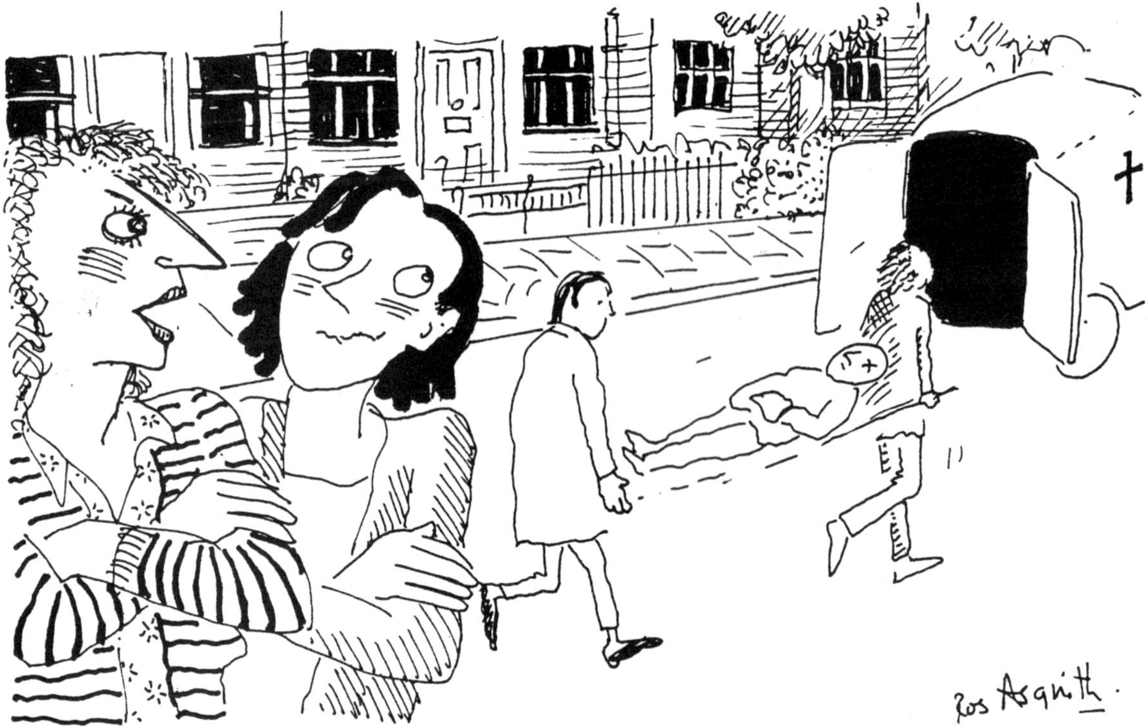
Ros Asquith

*"He said my soffits were sagging. So I hit him."*

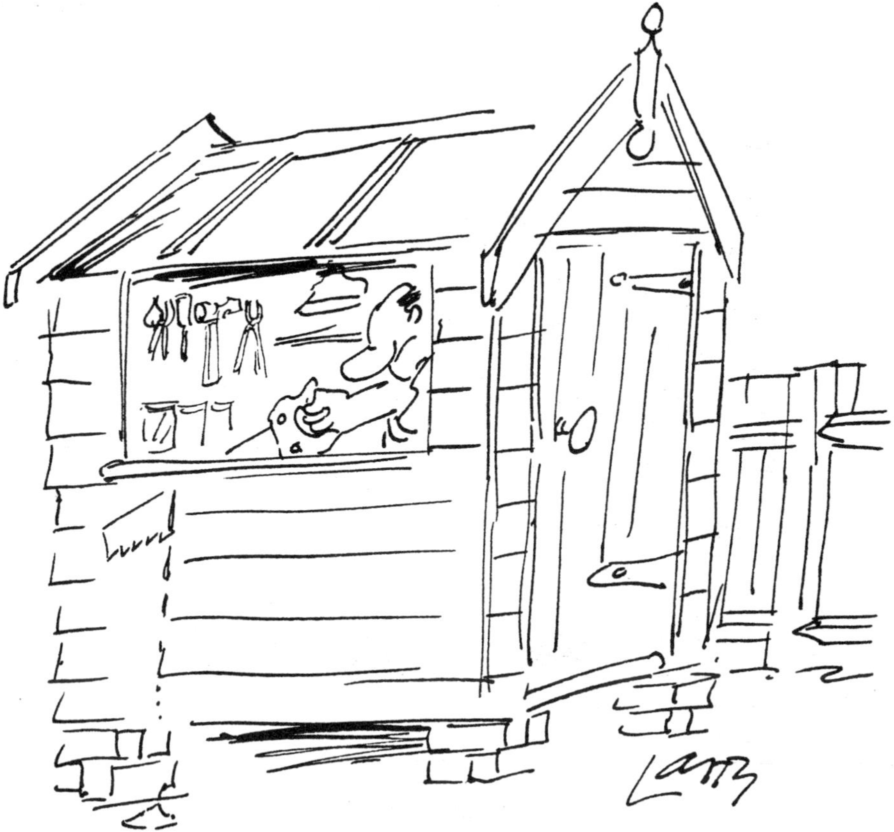

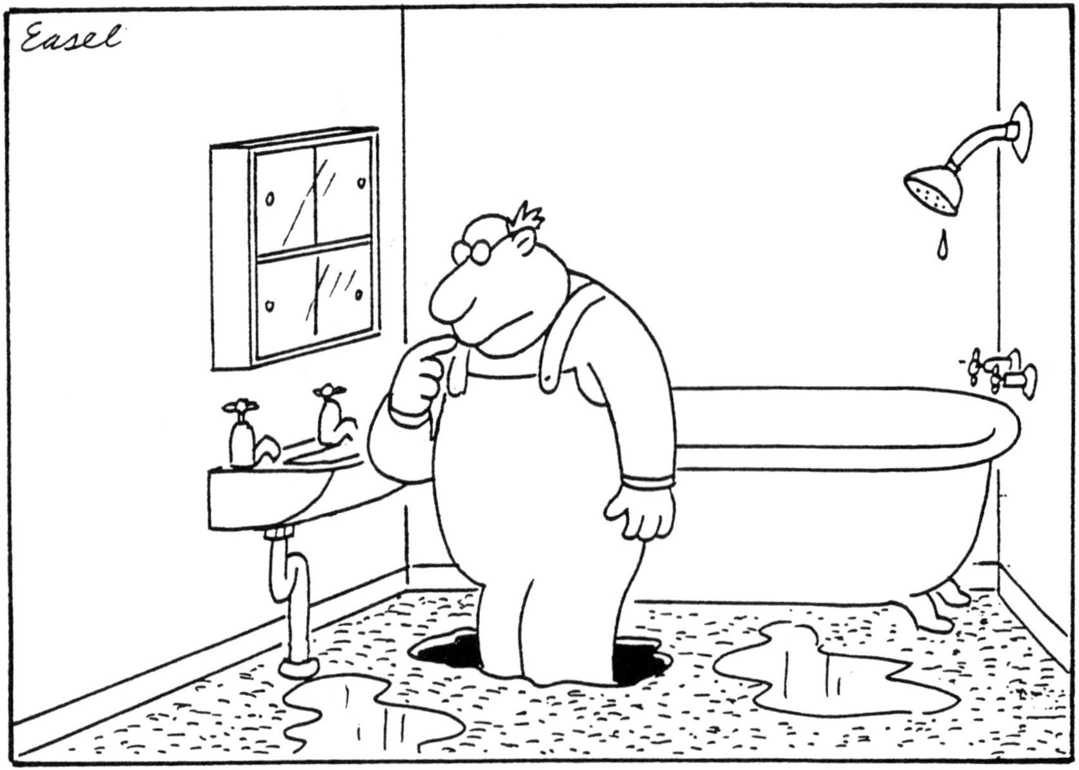
Easel

*Stan realized that it was probably not a good idea to have used chipboard flooring in the bathroom.*

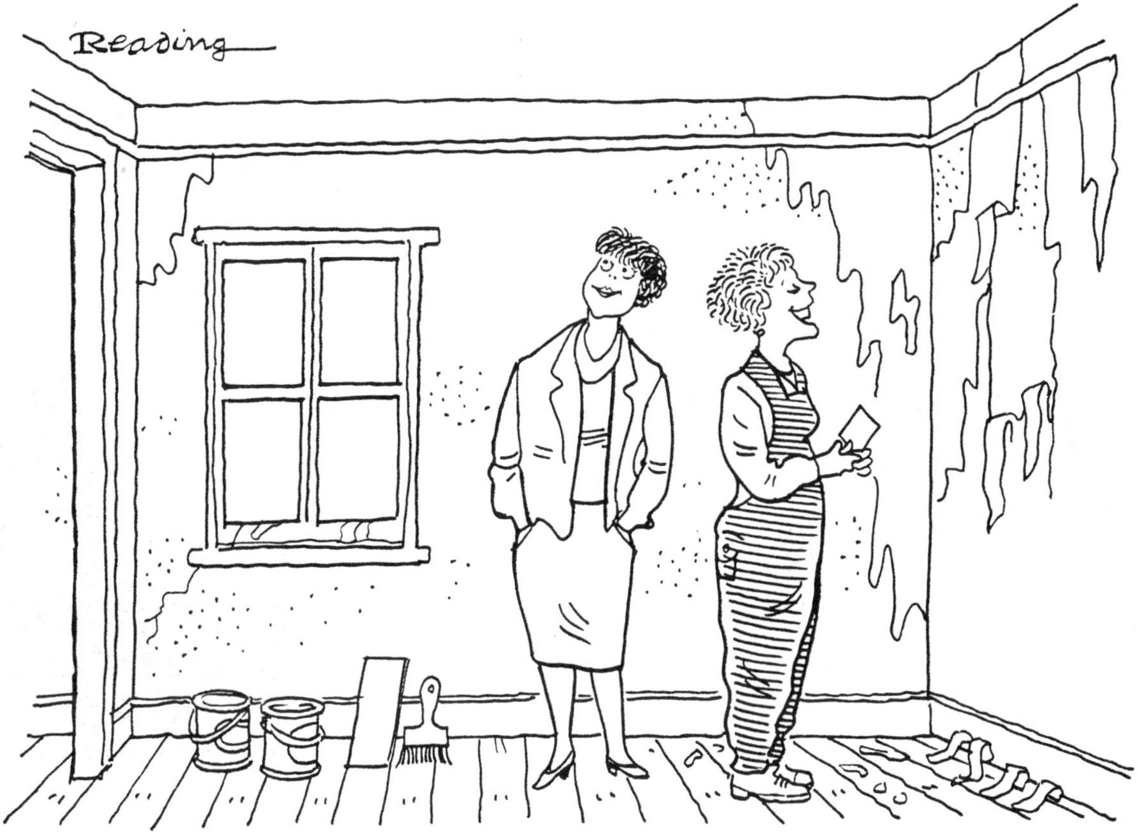
Reading

*"I could finish in a day, or two days if my husband helps."*

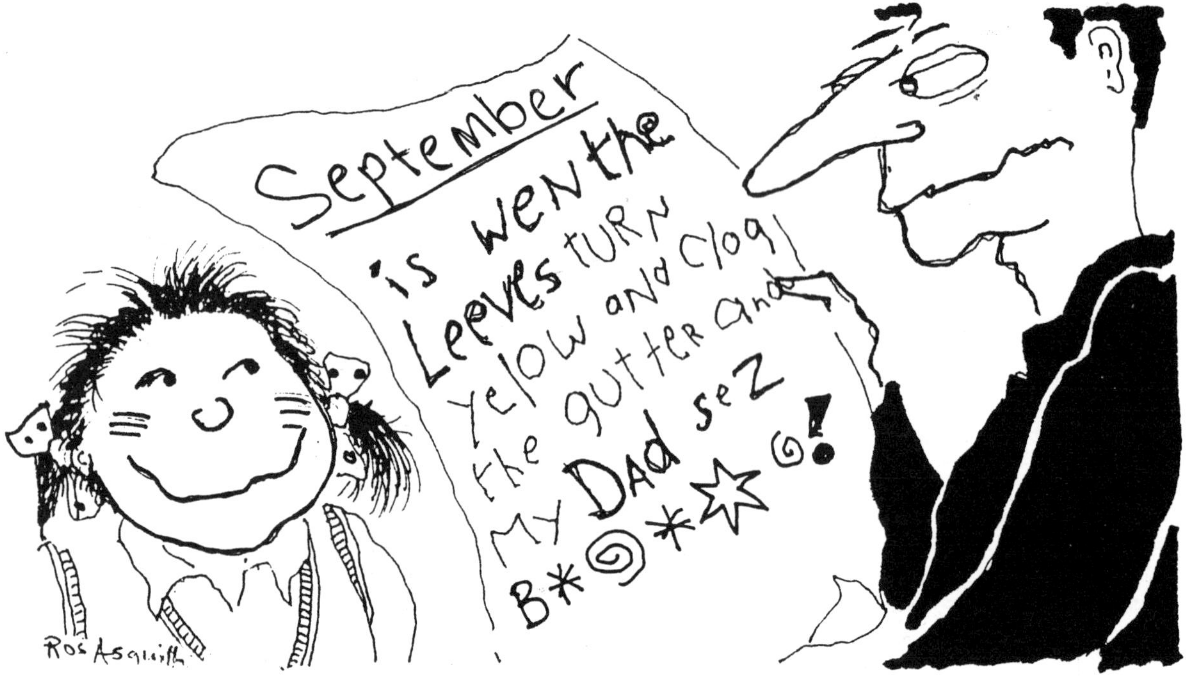
September
is wen the
Leeves turn
yelow and clog
the gutter and
my Dad sez
B*
Ros Asquith

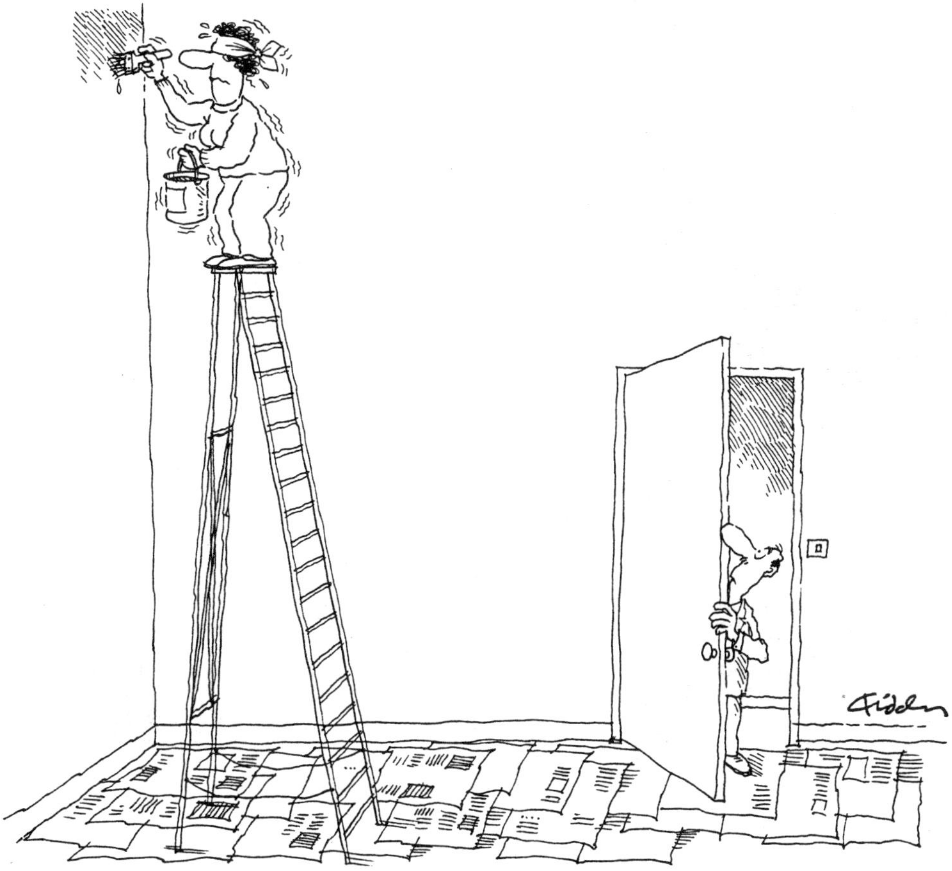

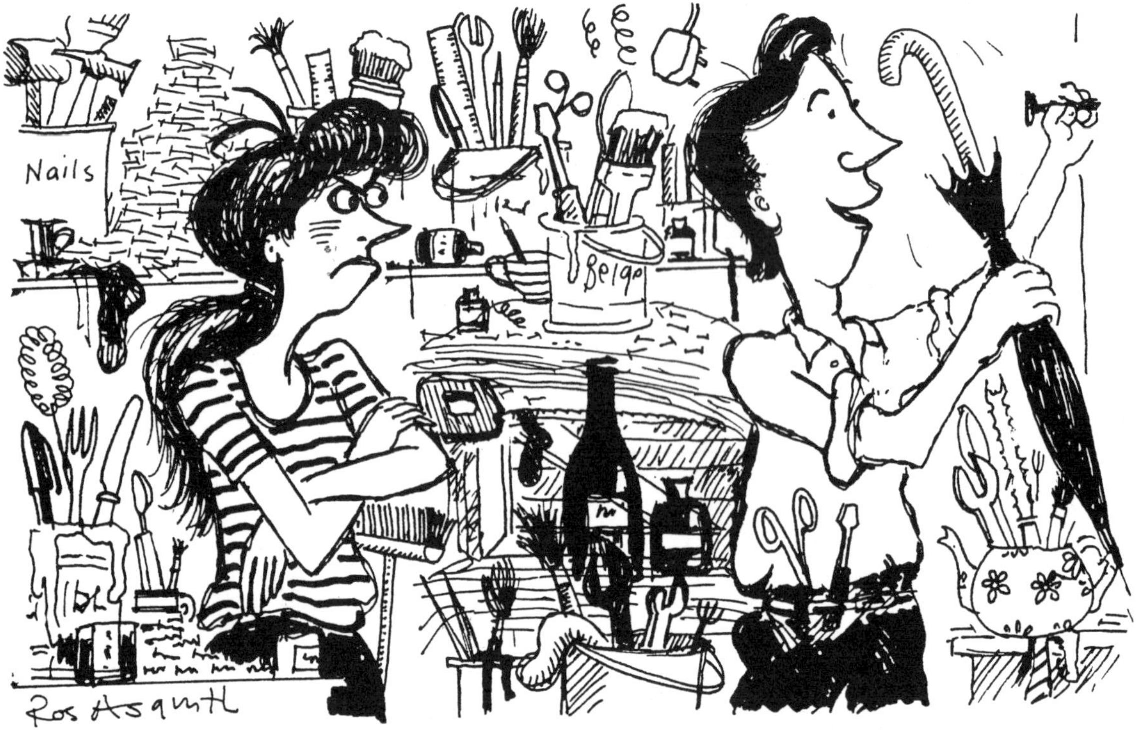
Nails
Belgo
Ros Asquith

*"Have you seen I've been tidying up?"*

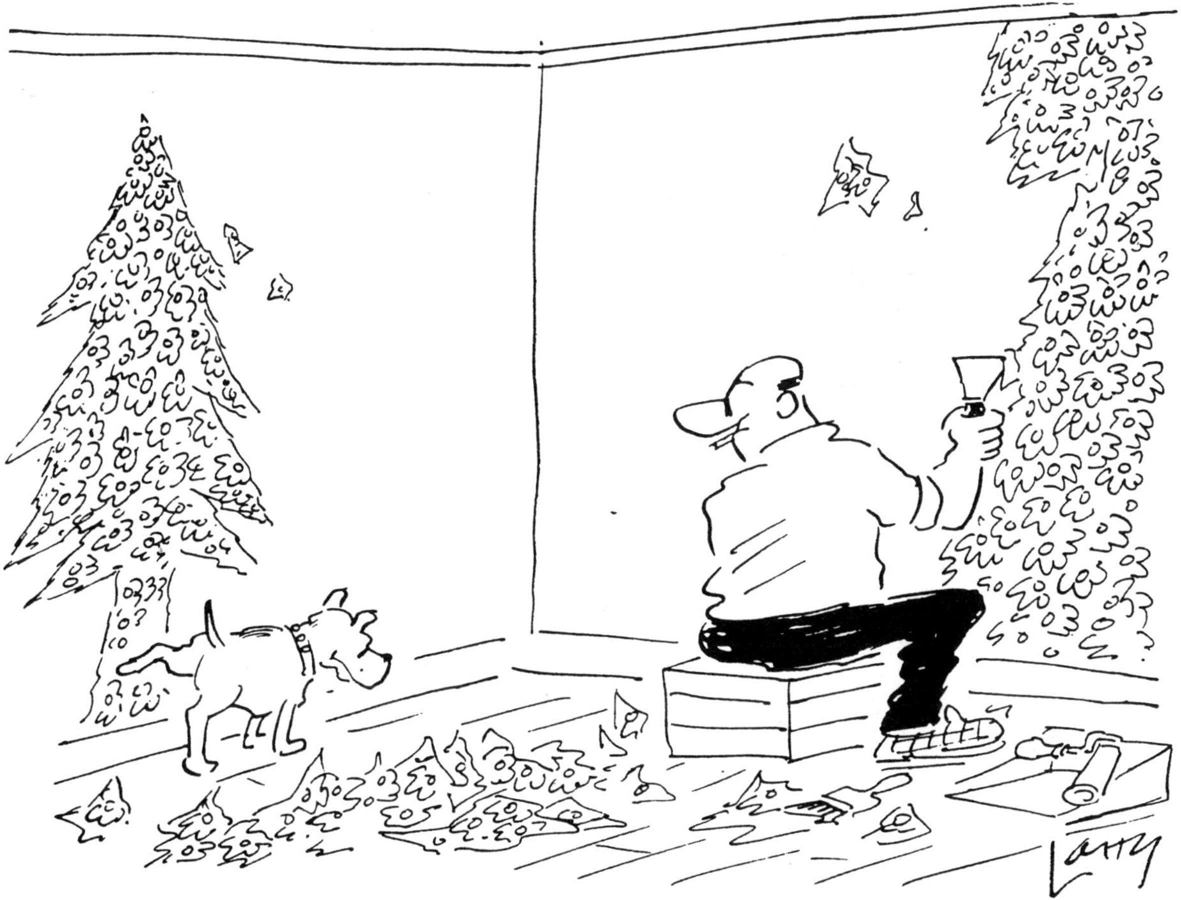

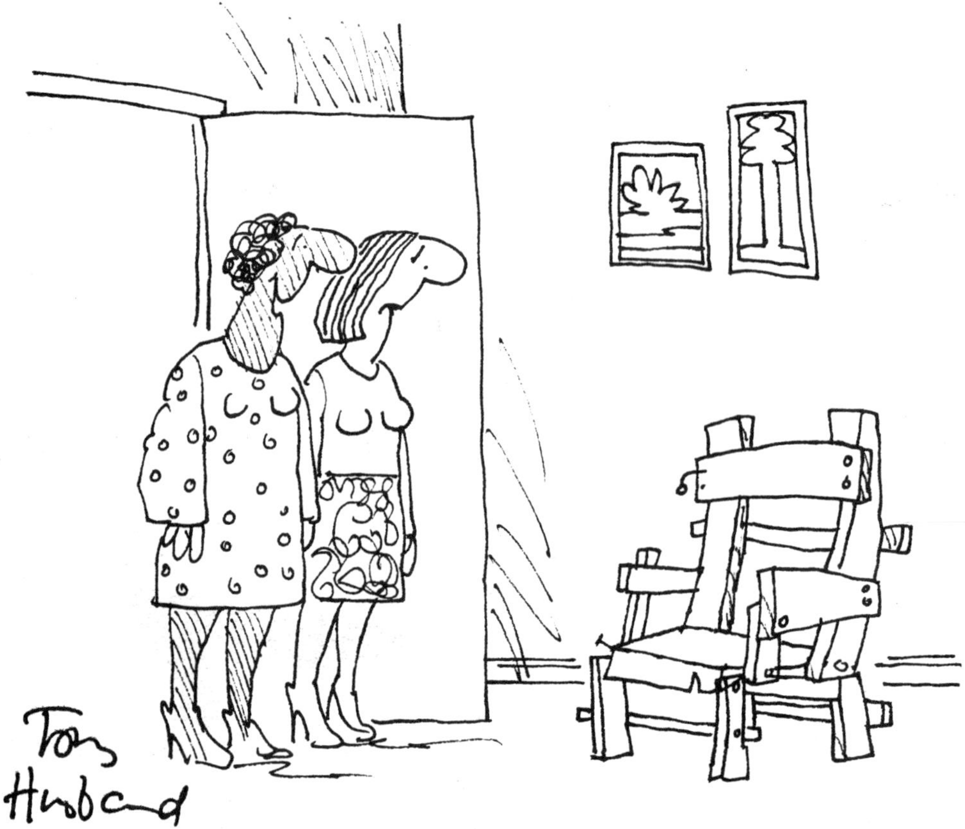

*"My husband made that chair."*

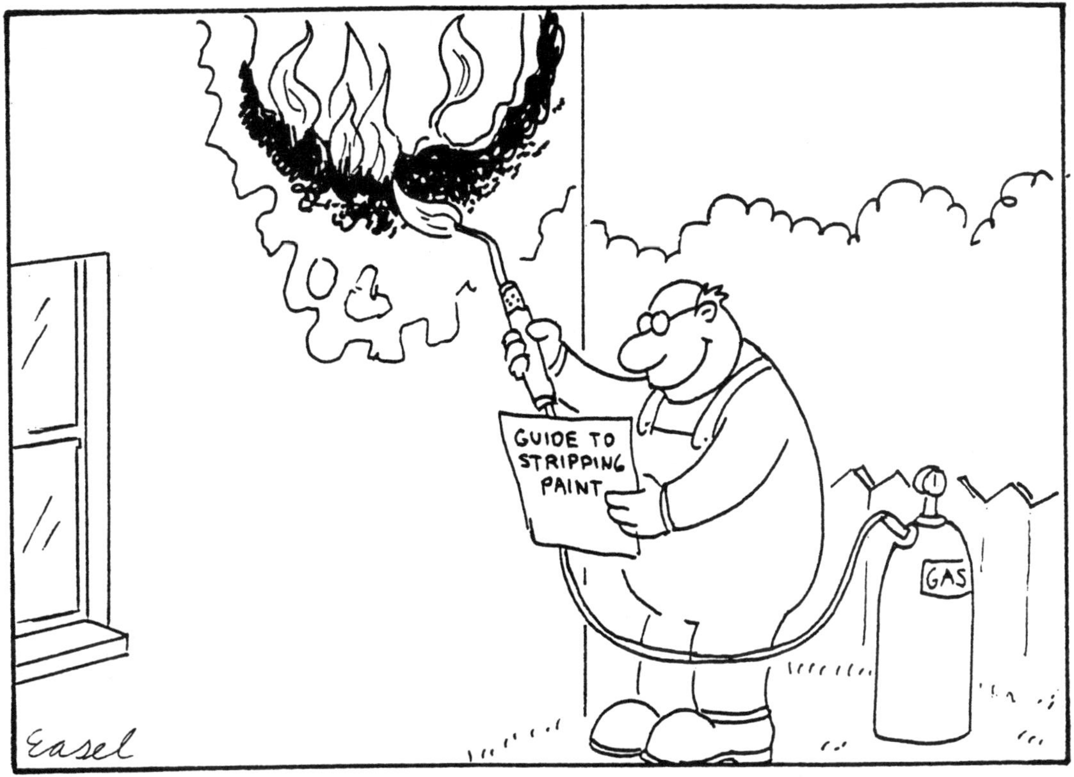
GUIDE TO STRIPPING PAINT
GAS
Easel

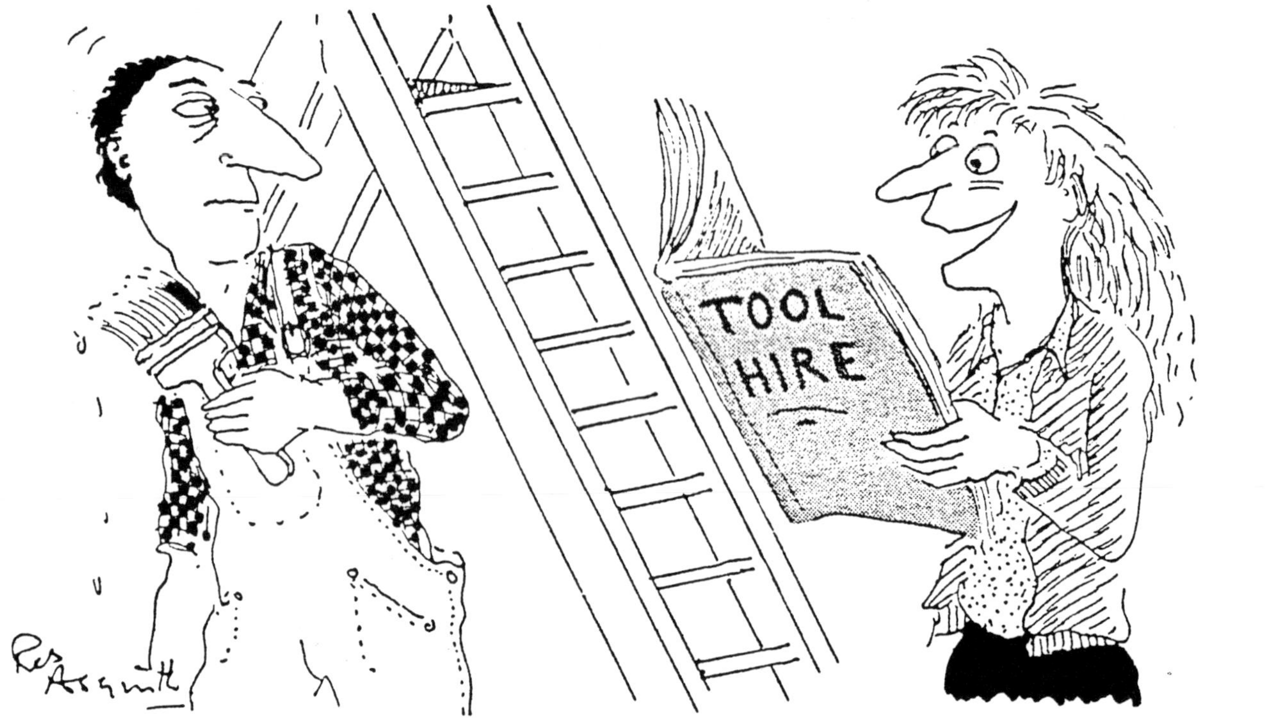
TOOL HIRE

*"You know that floor that took you three months?*
*– There's a tool in here does it in a couple of days."*

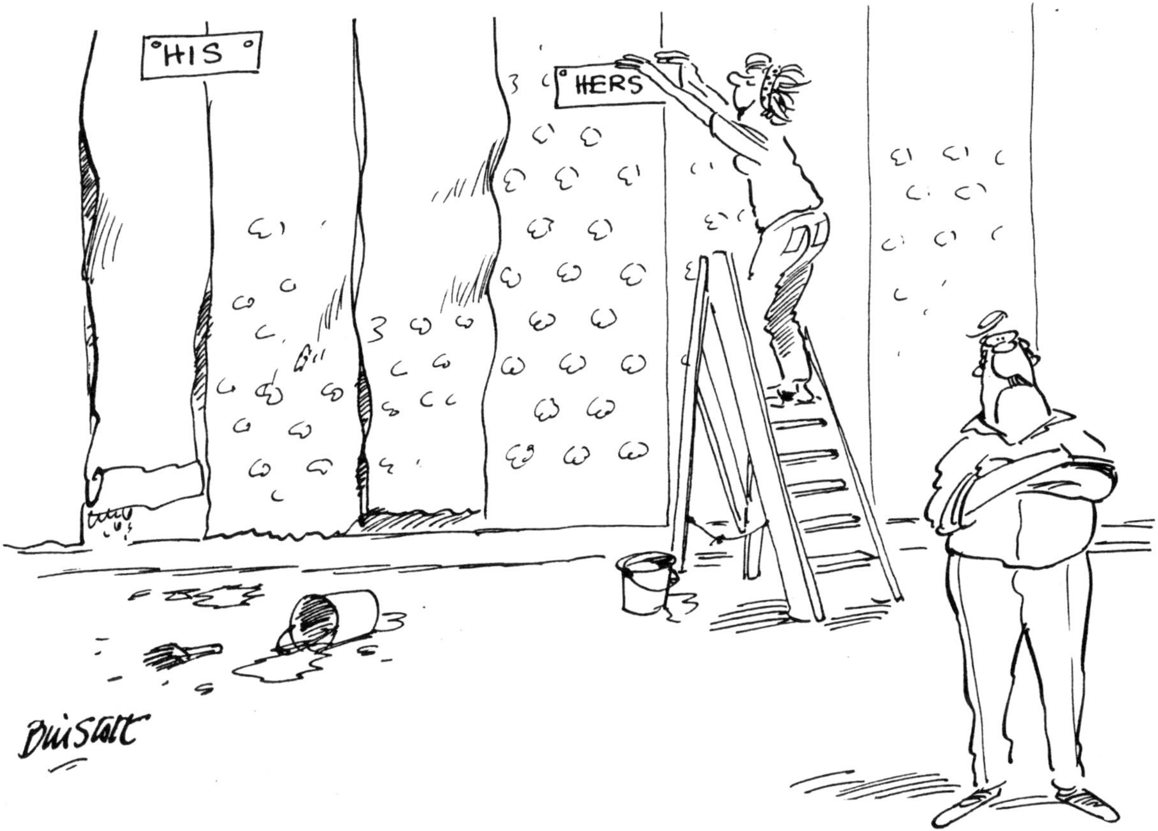
HIS
HERS

"OK, OK, you win. Your paper-hanging is better than mine."

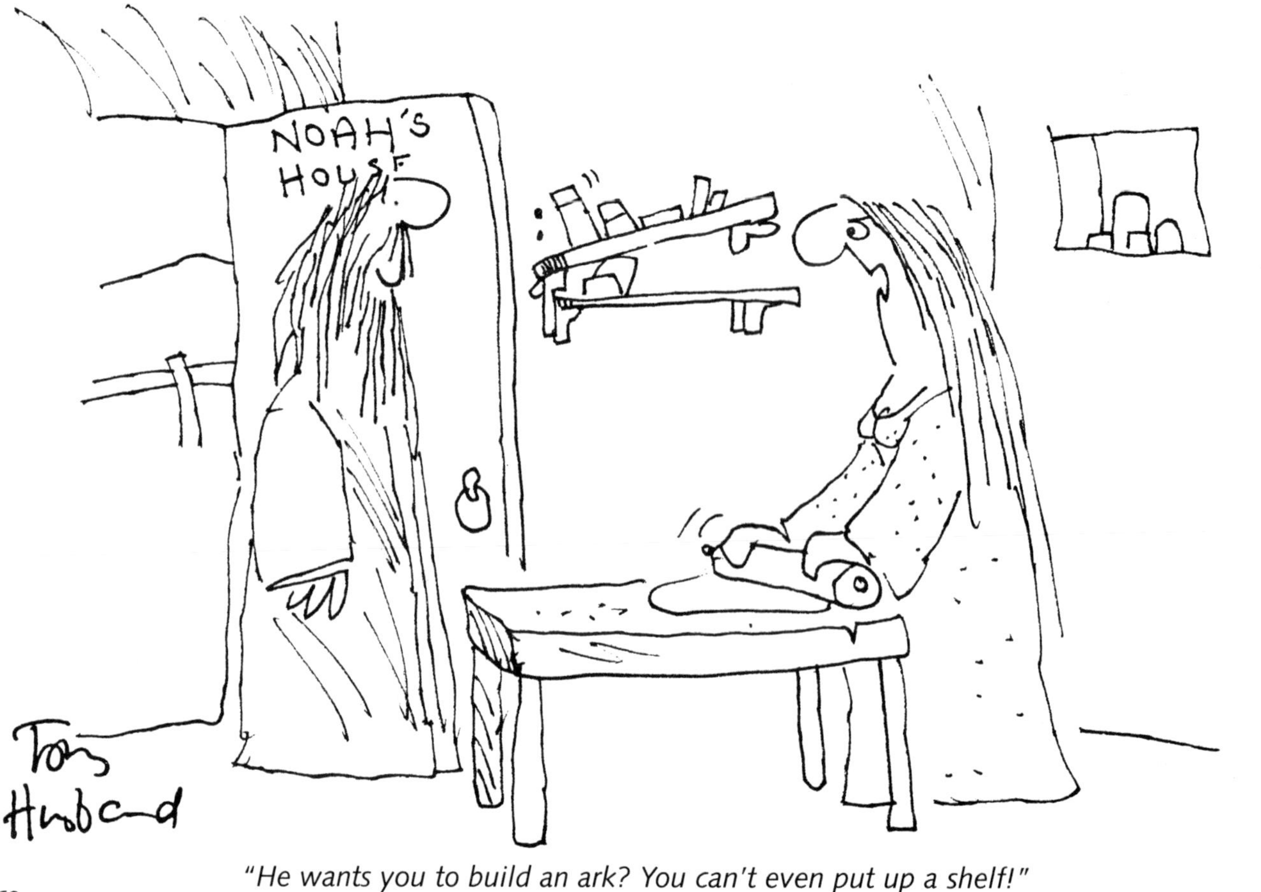
NOAH'S HOUSE
Tom Hubbard

*"He wants you to build an ark? You can't even put up a shelf!"*

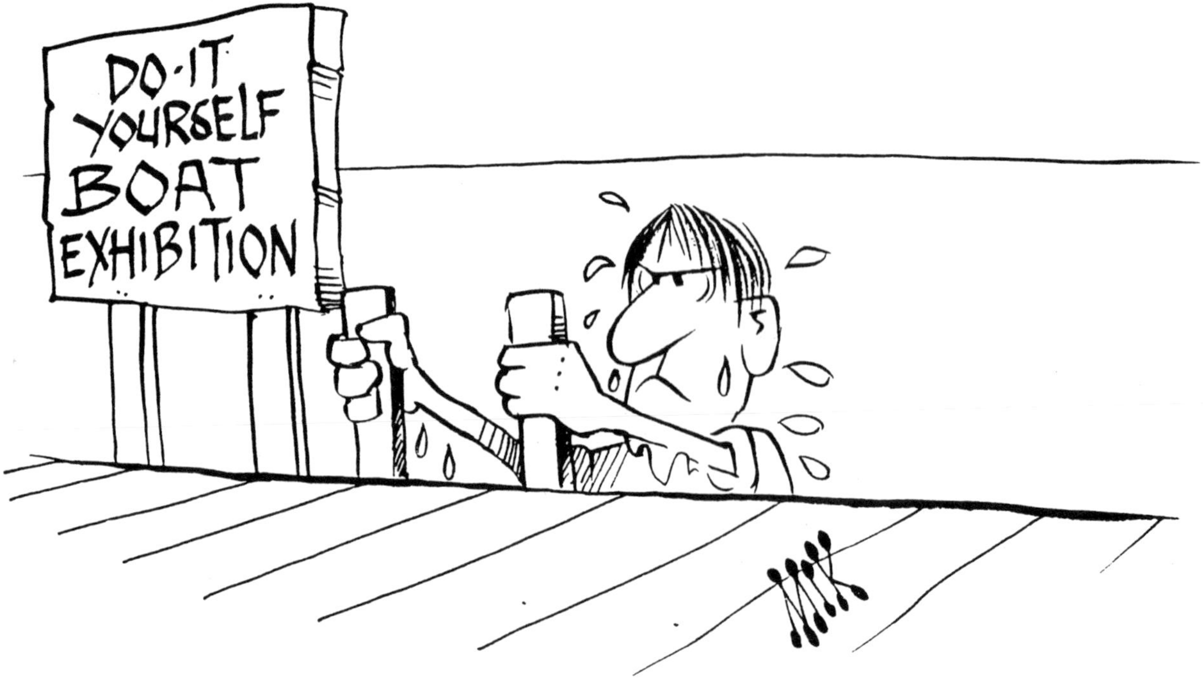
DO-IT YOURSELF BOAT EXHIBITION

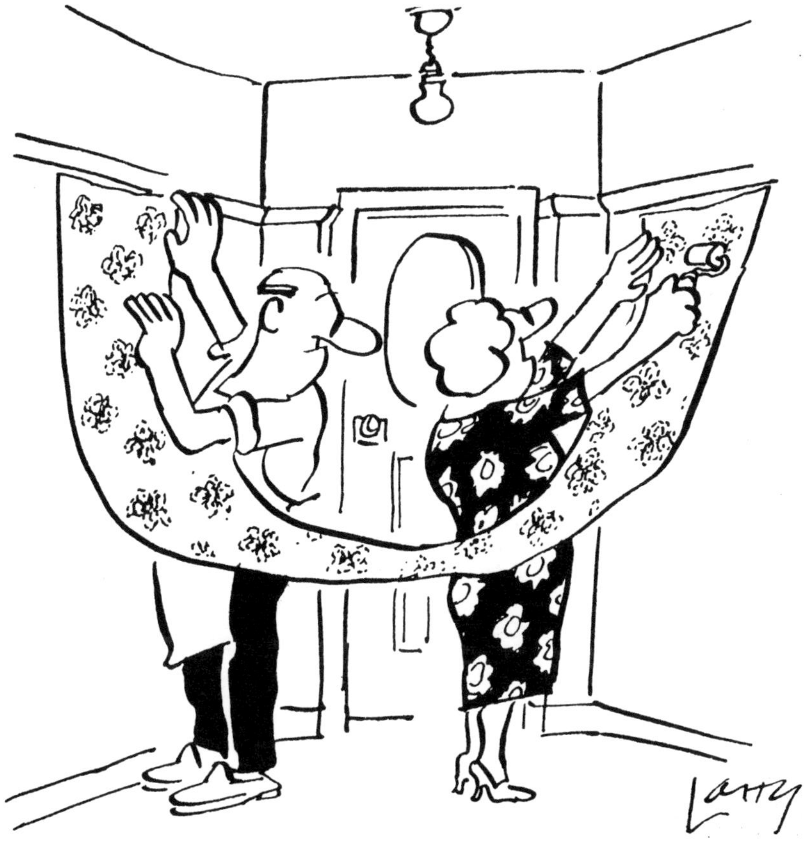
Larry

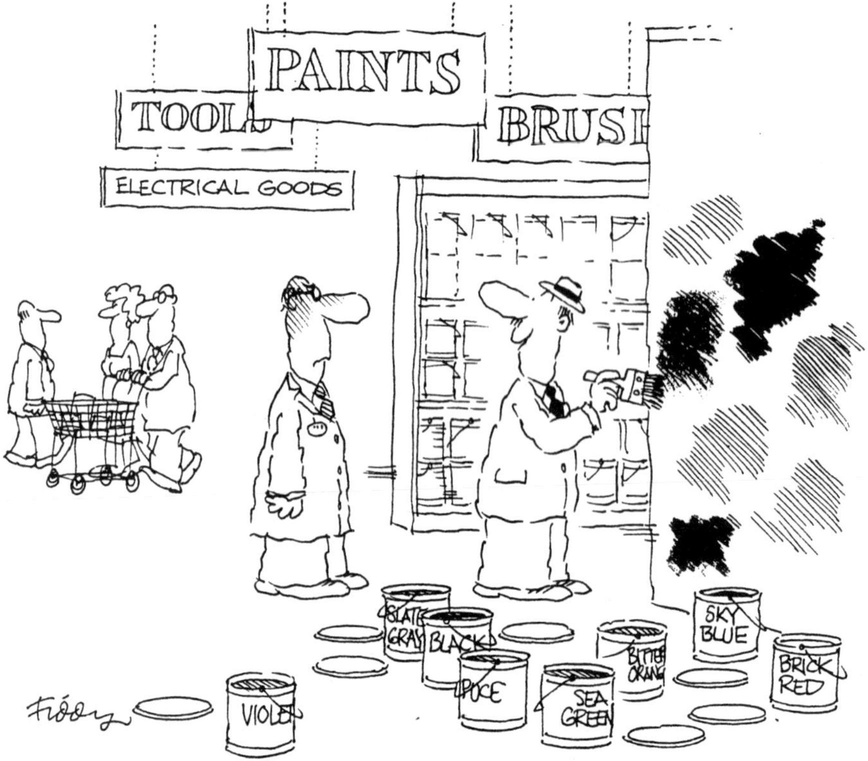
PAINTS
TOOLS
BRUSH
ELECTRICAL GOODS
SLATE GRAY
BLACK
PUCE
VIOLET
SEA GREEN
SKY BLUE
BRICK RED
Fiddy

*"No thanks – I'm just browsing."*

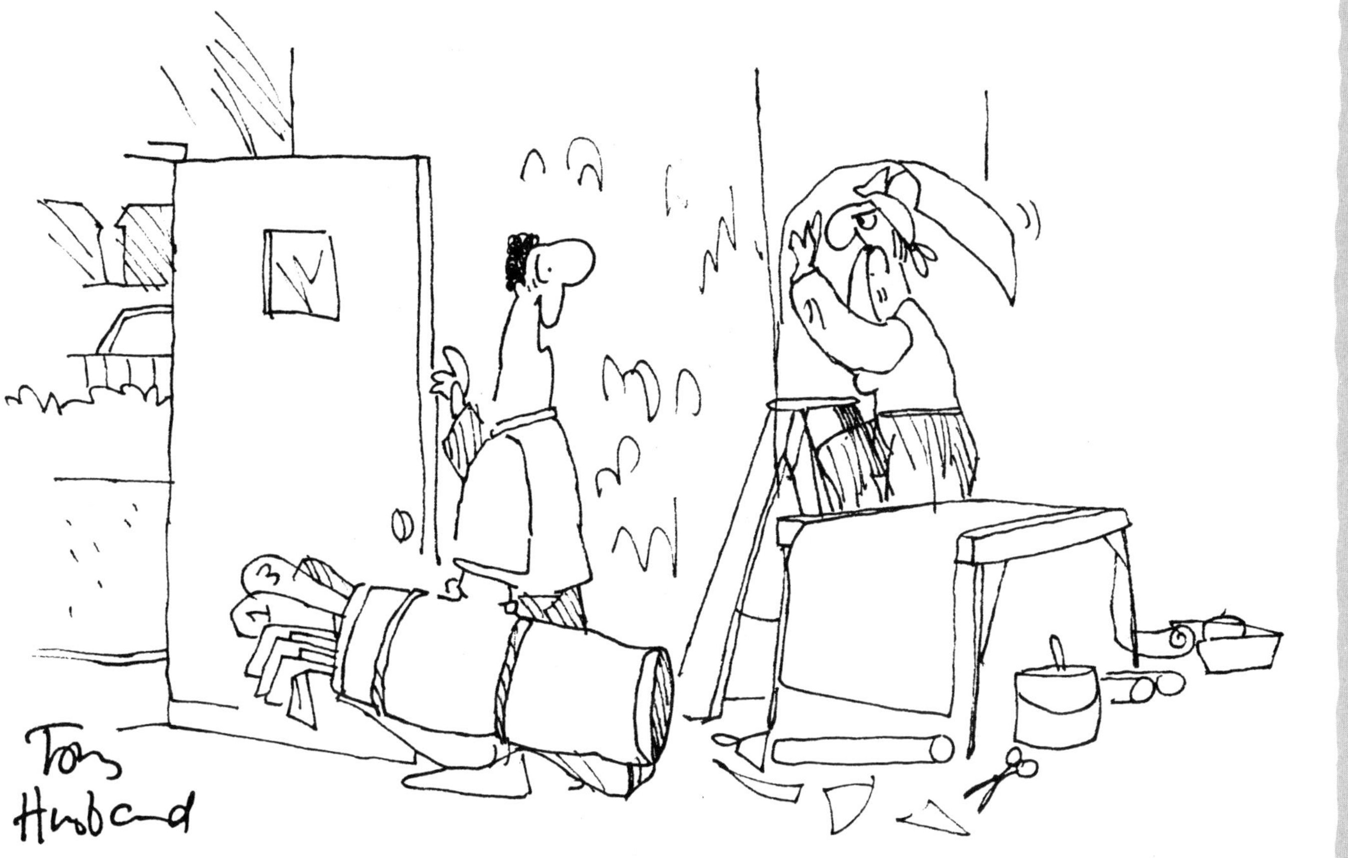

*"Right, I'm off now. See you later. . . OK?"*

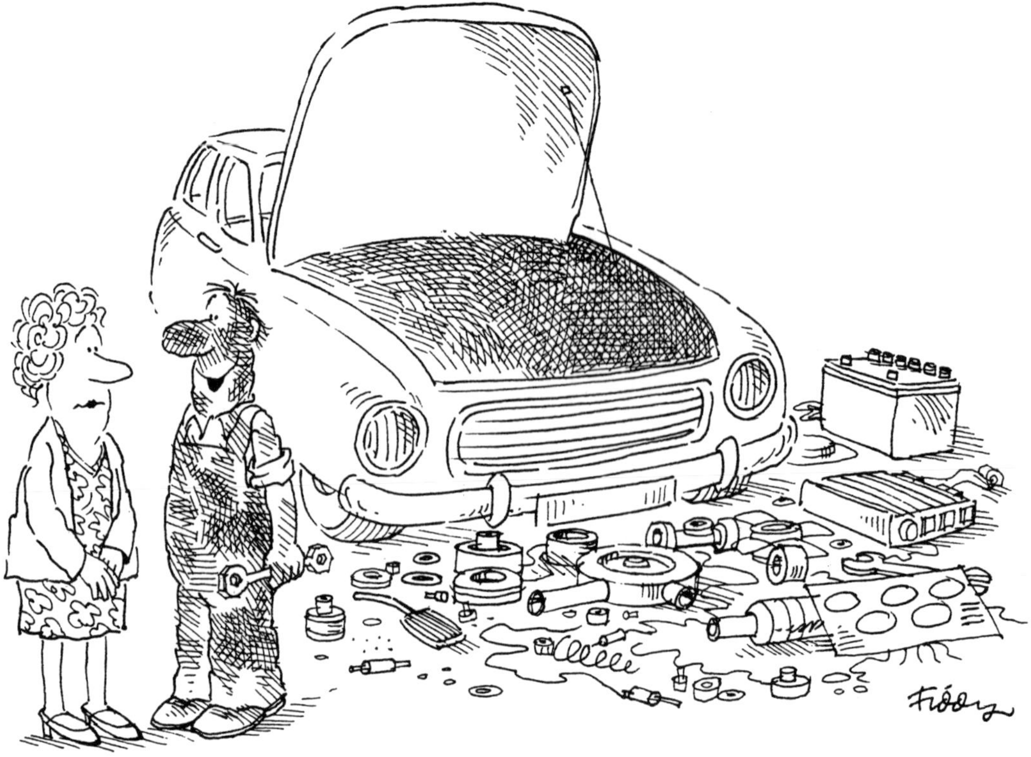

*"So far, so good!"*

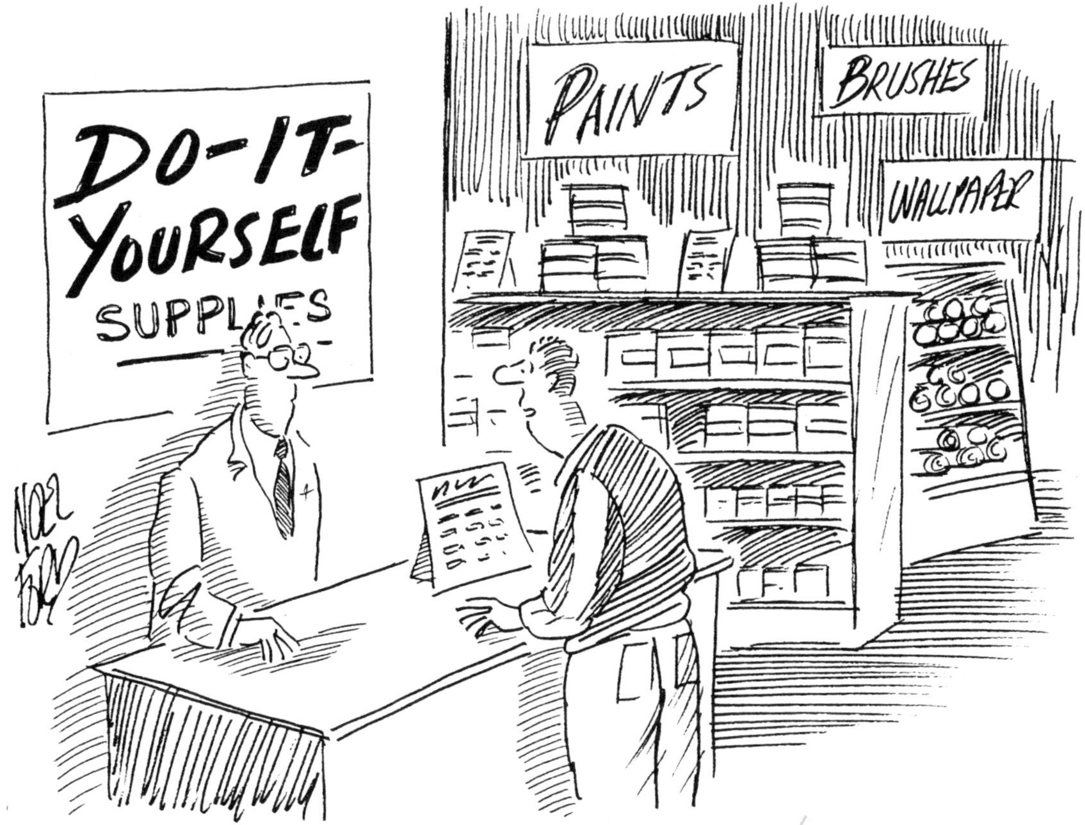
DO-IT-
YOURSELF
SUPPLIES
PAINTS
BRUSHES
WALLPAPER
NOEL FORD

*". . . and what do you have by way of GET-SOMEONE-ELSE-TO-DO-IT-FOR-YOU materials?"*

"How's it going, Michelangelo?"

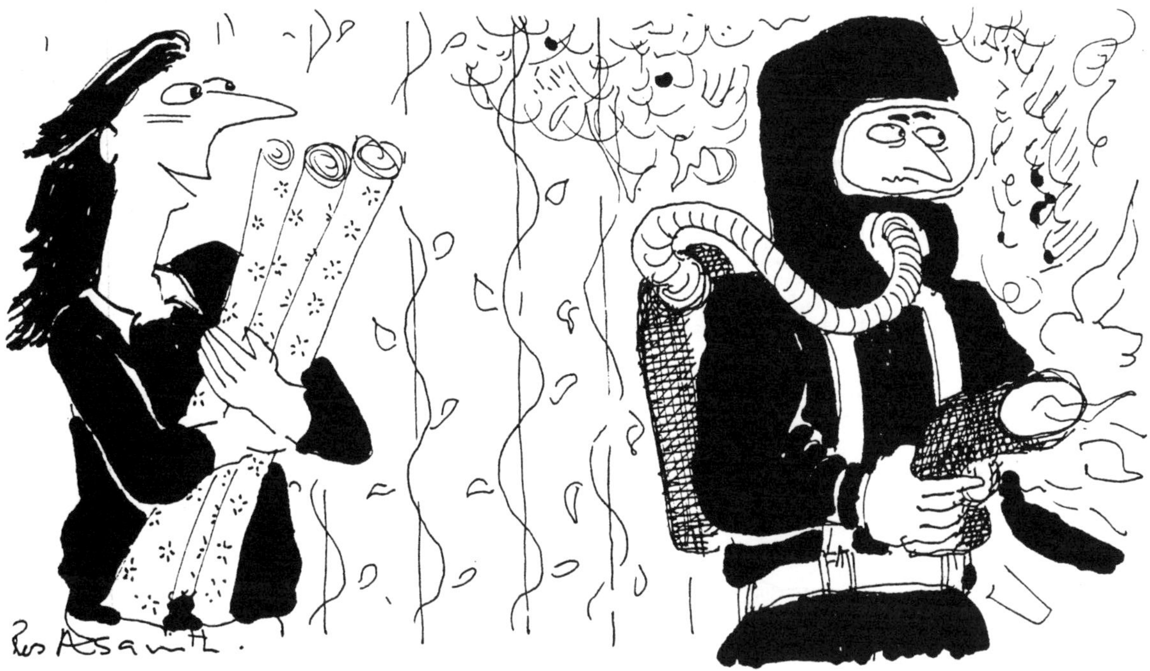

"OK, Red Adair, where do you want the new wallpaper?"

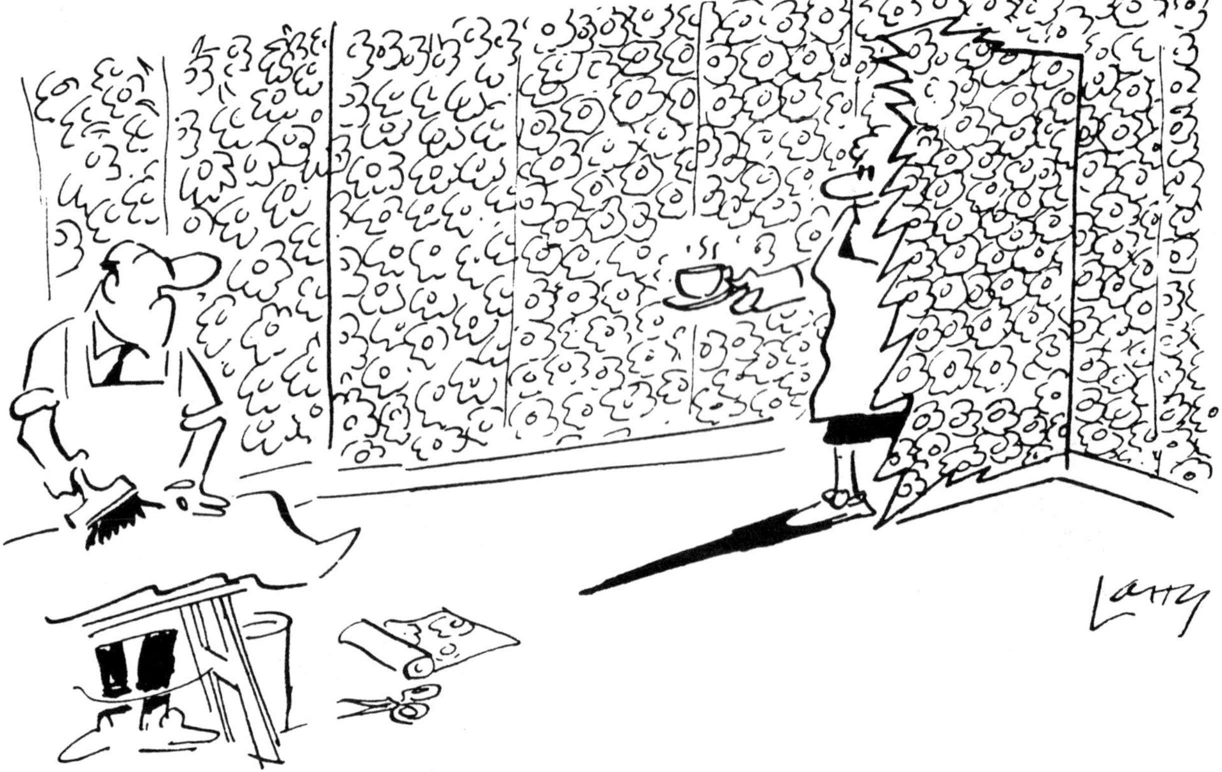
Larry

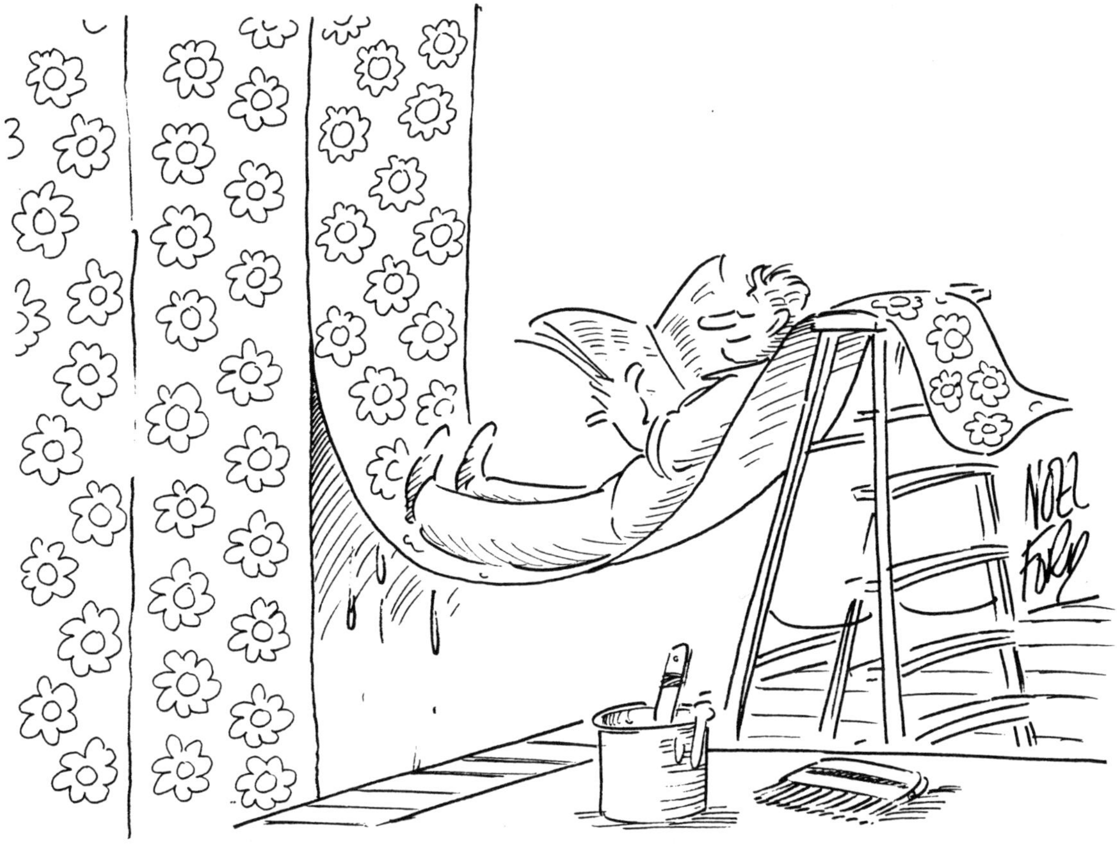
NOEL FORD

## Books in "The World's Greatest" series

($4.99 £2.99 paperback)

The World's Greatest Business Cartoons
The World's Greatest Cat Cartoons
The World's Greatest Computer Cartoons
The World's Greatest Dad Cartoons
The World's Greatest Do It Yourself Cartoons
The World's Greatest Golf Cartoons
The World's Greatest Keep-Fit Cartoons

## Books in the "Victim's Guide" series

($4.99 £2.99 paperback)

Award winning cartoonist Roland Fiddy sees the funny side
to life's phobias, nightmares and catastrophes.

The Victim's Guide to Air Travel
The Victim's Guide to the Baby
The Victim's Guide to Christmas
The Victim's Guide the Dentist
The Victim's Guide to the Doctor
The Victim's Guide to Middle Age

## Books in the "Crazy World" series

($4.99 £2.99 paperback)
The Crazy World of Aerobics (Bill Stott)
The Crazy World of Cats (Bill Stott)
The Crazy World of Cricket (Bill Stott)
The Crazy World of Gardening (Bill Stott)
The Crazy World of Golf (Mike Knowles)
The Crazy World of The Handyman (Roland Fiddy)
The Crazy World of Hospitals (Bill Stott)
The Crazy World of Housework (Bill Stott)
The Crazy World of The Learner Driver (Bill Stott)

The Crazy World of Love (Roland Fiddy)
The Crazy World of Marriage (Bill Stott)
The Crazy World of Rugby (Bill Stott)
The Crazy World of Sailing (Peter Rigby)
The Crazy World of School (Bill Stott)
The Crazy World of Sex (Bill Stott)
The Crazy World of Soccer (Bill Stott)

## Books in the "Fanatics" series

($4.99 £2.99 paperback)

The **Fanatic's Guides** are perfect presents for everyone
with a hobby that has got out of hand. Eighty pages of
hilarious black and white cartoons by Roland Fiddy.

The Fanatic's Guide to the Bed
The Fanatic's Guide to Cats
The Fanatic's Guide to Computers
The Fanatic's Guide to Dads
The Fanatic's Guide to Diets
The Fanatic's Guide to Dogs
The Fanatic's Guide to Husbands
The Fanatic's Guide to Money
The Fanatic's Guide to Sex
The Fanatic's Guide to Skiing
The Fanatic's Guide to Sports

**Great Britain:** Order these super books from your local
bookseller or from Exley Publications Ltd. 16 Chalk Hill,
Watford, Herts WDI 4BN. (Please send £1.30 to cover post
and packaging on 1 book, £2.60 on 2 or more books.)